THE TRAIL
OF THE SERPENT

The true story of a Victorian murder
on the London to Brighton railway line

JAMES GARDNER

In memory of Jimmie Gardner, my uncle

James Gardner has worked as a teacher in London and Italy. He now lives near Brighton and works part-time in the mental health field. His well received first book, *Sweet Bells Jangled Out of Tune*, was a history of the former Sussex Lunatic Asylum at Haywards Heath.

Published by Pomegranate Press
51 St Nicholas Lane, Lewes, Sussex BN7 2JZ
email: pomegranatepress@aol.com

ISBN 0-9542587-6-2

British Library Cataloguing-in-Publication Data.
A catalogue record for this book is available from the British Library.

Printed by Biddles Ltd, 24 Rollesby Road, King's Lynn, Norfolk PE30 4LS

ACKNOWLEDGEMENTS

First and foremost I owe a debt to a local journalist, Dianne Jones, who encouraged me to write the book and who substantially improved the early drafts by her editing and suggestions. I must also thank the following people for reading various manuscripts and for their very valuable criticisms and suggestions: Vic Baines, Janice Balfour, Anne Blyton, Victoria Caldarola, Barbara Dale, Kerry Doyle, Jane Edwards, Roger Gardner, John Lewell, Erica Macdonald-Gibson, Mireille Mello, Sharon Mills, Jeannet Renfree, Geoffrey Simmons, Juliette Smith, Adam Trimingham, Paul Turner, Marilyn Vrabez and Martin Walsh.

I am also indebted to Gail O'brien who supplied me with valuable research and to Colleen Eldredge, Vicki Gardner and Penny Hawkins who did likewise. Thanks also to Professor Joe Sim for advice about sources on Victorian prisons. Many thanks to Eddie Howlands who designed a very good publicity poster for the story. In addition I owe a debt to Mr T. Knight of Lewes prison who gave me a tour of the prison and provided me with some useful information.

Special thanks are also due to Dr Richard Wheeler, formerly head of St Francis Hospital, Haywards Heath, for his observations on Lefroy's state of mind. I must also thank staff of Madame Tussauds, the Covent Garden Theatre Museum, the Public Records Office, East Sussex Record Office, Carlisle Record Office, the National Newspaper Library at Colindale and the Brighton Local History Library. I would like to thank Madame Tussauds for giving me permission to reproduce the display picture of Lefroy.

Great thanks to David Arscott for his help, advice and skill in editing and producing this book and for his enduring patience. Finally, I would like to thank my brother, Steve Gardner, who once again has offered incredible support both practical and otherwise in the development of this book.

NOTE ON SOURCES

This is a true story. In order to recreate the atmosphere of the time I have extensively used contemporary newspapers and magazines. To avoid constantly quoting sources I have on occasion paraphrased articles.

PREFACE

Henry Mapleton was an ambitious 19th century Royal Navy officer who narrowly failed to make the grade. It wasn't that he lacked ability or professional competence (11 years of continual service and promotion are proof of that), but after a promising start he suffered more than his fair share of misfortune.

Mapleton joined up on February 23rd 1825. He was just 15. He was assigned to a 42-gun ship, *Doris*, and before long became the youngest master in the Royal Navy. In 1835 the famous explorer Captain Sir James Clark Ross was commissioned by Hull ship owners to relieve whaling ships stuck in the Arctic ice. For this dangerous mission Ross chose Mapleton as his second master on the *Cove*. At the end of the year-long voyage Ross recommended him for promotion. In 1839 the Royal Geographical Society and the Admiralty despatched a two-boat expedition under Ross to explore the Antarctic and he was offered a salary of £100 a year to be the master. Unfortunately, Mapleton caught yellow fever at the last moment and was unable to go, so losing out on what turned out to be an historic voyage.

The following year he was sponsored by merchants to explore the Antarctic in the *Eliza Scott* but lost his rudder in a terrible storm and was forced to take refuge on the solitary island of St Helena in the South Atlantic. After the boat was repaired it was hired out for charter. On one occasion, when Mapleton was about to set sail for the Cape of Good Hope, a ship arrived from the Ascension Island with news of a severe drought there. He decided to forfeit his charter and, at his own expense, bought casks and filled them with water and set sail for that island. He arrived just in time to save the islanders from dying of thirst. As a reward they presented him with a giant turtle and he was granted an extension of leave by the Admiralty. Although recent research has revealed that they were heavily overcharged for their water, some considered that Mapleton was poorly rewarded for his heroism.

Deciding to settle in St Helena, he soon became harbour master and was promoted to staff commander. He was married there and had two daughters. In 1862, he retired on half-pay and returned to England. He drank heavily in his later years and died in 1879. A.G.E. Jones, in his book *Polar Portraits*, records that he left less than £200, some property and a life policy to his two daughters. In his account of Henry Mapleton's life, Jones surprisingly fails to mention the fact that he also had a son – a son who had been born 35 years to the day since Mapleton joined the navy and whose name, two years after Henry's death, would both shock and fascinate late Victorian society.

This is his story.

CONTENTS

To the Education Officer at Lewes Prison
8th April 1978

Dear Sir,

I was 101 years old last February 2nd and since then I've had some mixed memories of something which happened while I was living at the Sussex Militia Barracks at Southover, Lewes. My father, Mr Edward Lawson, was in charge of the Sussex Militia.

I remember my mother telling the older ones to listen to the prison bells, a man . . . had been hanged that morning because he had killed someone in the tunnel of a train near Lewes. The prison was higher up than Southover and sounded plainly.

I'm terribly sorry to trouble you, but I thought you could tell me if any of my memories are real, because a 100 years is a long time to remember so vividly.

Mabel S. Whiting

PART ONE

A HIDEOUS CRIME

1

Preston Park Station, Brighton, Monday June 27th, 1881.

A howling whistle pierced the silence of the sultry afternoon. Two uniformed figures ambled out from the shade of a building and stood on the edge of a platform. Sweating profusely, they directed their eyes to the right. Shimmering heat from the rails distorted the outline of the two o'clock express from London Bridge as it came into view.

Gradually the familiar choking noise of the engine grew louder and louder until the men felt the platform rumble and shudder beneath them. One of the ticket collectors, Joseph Starks, started to run alongside the train as it pulled in. As he did so, his colleague, Richard Gibson, thought he saw a passenger with his head out of a compartment window shouting out something. Amidst the screeching of brakes and jets of steam the train suddenly halted.

Starks collected from the front of the train. On opening the door of a first class compartment, he found, sitting all alone, a man with his head held down.

'Tickets please, sir,' requested Starks.

The man did not respond.

'Let me see your ticket please, sir,' Starks repeated.

Preston Park station, 1890.

The man looked up. His face was covered in blood. Blood was also encrusted on his hair and forehead and drenched his shirt and jacket. Brushing Starks aside, he stumbled from the compartment onto the platform in a dazed and almost hysterical state.

'Look here, I've been attacked!' he blurted out. 'Shot at. Is there a policeman here? I need a doctor. I need a wash.'

Starks shouted to Gibson in the next carriage.

'Dick, call the stationmaster. A man's been attacked.'

Starks looked back into the compartment and saw a pool of blood on the floor under the man's seat.

'Someone tried to kill me!' the man exclaimed. 'I feel very faint. I need water. Is there a doctor nearby?'

Starks tried to calm him down. At the same time other passengers began to leave their compartments and wander down the platform towards them. The stationmaster, Henry Anscombe, rushed up with Gibson and told them to return to their seats.

Anscombe studied the compartment. There was blood on the seats, the cushions and the rope mats covering the floor. He turned and looked at the agitated man stumbling about on the platform. He was young and very thin with a wispy stubble on his chin. Blood was still oozing from his head. The man removed his hat and showed the stationmaster his wounds.

'When I entered the train at London Bridge,' he explained, 'there was an elderly, prosperous looking man and a rough looking countryman, aged about 50, in the compartment. They didn't speak to me or to each other. Just as the train entered the tunnel after Croydon I was fired at and then hit over the head and made unconscious.'

'Who by?' asked Anscombe.

' I'm sure it was the countryman.'

'Where is he now?'

'He must have got off at another station.'

The stationmaster looked surprised.

'But this train doesn't stop between here and Croydon.'

'He must have jumped out then.'

'What about the other gentleman?

The passenger shrugged his shoulders. The officials looked mystified. No one had passed through their ticket barrier. Nor was there anyone on board who answered the descriptions he had given. Anscombe told Gibson to take him to the mainline station at Brighton. He could tell his tale to the railway police there.

As the passenger began to get back into the carriage, the guard, Thomas Watson, noticed something odd about him. He had a chain hanging out of his shoe. Watson bent down and pulled it out. Attached to it was a gold watch.

'What's this here?'

The man looked surprised.

'Oh, I don't know how it got there.'

Watson handed it back to him.

During the mile-long journey to Brighton the injured passenger calmed down and even pointed out of the window at some beautiful scenery. He asked several times if he could see a doctor, claiming that it was 'cruel to keep me in this state'. Gibson noticed his collar was missing and that his head was still bleeding. He checked his ticket and asked for his address. The man courteously handed him a blood-stained calling card.

> ARTHUR LEFROY,
> AUTHOR AND JOURNALIST
> 4 Cathcart Road, Wallington, Surrey

At Brighton Station it was decided that Lefroy should be sent with Gibson and a railway policeman, Martin, to the police station. There he made a statement to a clerk, giving the details of the assault. He said he had come to Brighton to see Mrs Nye Chart, a well known theatre proprietor, about producing a play he had written. Martin was sent to check the story but she was not at home.

After a long wait in vain for the police doctor, the clerk told Gibson and Martin to take Lefroy – with blood still trickling down his forehead – by cab to the local hospital. During the journey he complained about his treatment and kept on asking how much further the hospital was. On their arrival a doctor, Benjamin Hall, bandaged his head and inquired about his wounds. Lefroy told him that he had been struck by a blunt instrument but was not sure what kind. Hall thought it looked as if a pistol or revolver had been pressed against his head. He suggested he stay the night at the hospital, but Lefroy said he could not as he had an urgent business appointment at his club in London that evening.

Martin and Gibson took him back to the police station. On the way, Lefroy asked Martin to stop the cab outside a shop and get him a new collar. Martin obliged and Lefroy gave him the money. He told the men that, as he had been robbed, he could not give them a tip but would soon be coming into money and would send them a 'handsome present' for their kindness.

At the police station, Lefroy was interviewed briefly by the chief constable of Brighton, James Terry, an avuncular man in his late fifties.

Two poorly dressed railway detectives, Howland and Holmes, stood by. Some false coins – bronze Hanoverian sovereigns – had been found on the floor of the train compartment. Were they his?

Lefroy thought they must have belonged to his assailant. He then complained indignantly about his treatment. Why had all the officials been more interested in questioning him for 'hours' instead of getting him the immediate medical attention he so desperately needed? He threatened to make an official complaint about their behaviour.

Terry apologised for the delay and said he knew Mrs Chart quite well and was sure she would see Lefroy tomorrow morning. Why didn't he stay the night? Not in the state he was in, came the reply, with his clothes all bloodied. Besides, he had to get back to London and go to his club.

Terry consulted the detectives. One of them had interviewed another passenger on the train, who told him that it had appeared to stop at Hassocks Gate a couple of miles north of Preston Park. He had got up to collect his luggage when the train had without warning moved off abruptly, almost knocking him over.

Terry decided to allow Lefroy to return home as long as he agreed to travel in the 'care' of Howland and Holmes. Lefroy readily consented and was escorted back to the railway station. He saw the stationmaster, Mr Anscombe, and told him he was 'hurt all over' and was 'desperate' to get home. Anscombe asked Holmes to search him. He had little of value on him apart from a few shillings and the gold watch.

Lefroy bought a ticket and boarded the 6.10 London train accompanied by Holmes, who sat with him while Howland sat in another part of the train. A few yards away the carriage containing the blood-stained compartment was shunted into a siding close to the goods yard, ready for a thorough examination by railway officials.

A First Class carriage on the London to Brighton line.

2

Two hours before Lefroy left Brighton, two railway platelayers, Thomas Jennings and his nephew, William, were checking the line for obstructions about 20 miles north of Brighton. The men, bare-chested and sweating heavily, were glad to enter the larder-like coolness of the mile-long Balcombe tunnel. Once inside the echoing pitch black chamber, they began to scour the line with their oil lamps.

About half-way along, Tom thought he could see a pile of clothes in the gap which divided the up track from the down. He lowered his lamp to take a closer look and discovered to his horror that it was the body of a man. He was lying on his back in a straight line parallel to the rail, with his head towards Brighton. Tom pulled away the corner of the jacket which obscured the man's head. The face was badly cut and covered in black dirt and dried blood. The right arm was clenched over his breast and his left fist was dug into the ballast. A thumb was almost severed. Tom placed his fingers on the man's heart. The body was still warm, but the man was clearly dead.

He called his young nephew over. Both stared at the body for a few seconds, then hurried back the way they had come towards the orange glow that marked the tunnel's entrance. Soon they met another platelayer, Stephen Williams, and told him of their grisly discovery. Williams asked the men to stay with the body and went to alert the Balcombe signal box. The information was telegraphed to London Bridge Station and, after a short delay, transmitted to other stations along the Brighton to London line. Curiously, the only stations not informed were Preston Park and Brighton.

As Tom and William waited they were joined by other workmen who came to look at the corpse. Soon the tunnel's walls were alive with the flickering shadows of burning oil lamps. One of the men found a spot where it looked as if someone had fallen down onto the line. Another thought the body appeared to have been dragged a short distance, especially as one of the man's boots was found 10 yards away. Others joked nervously about his possible fate.

At 7pm an engine and break arrived to take the body away to Balcombe Station. From there it was taken by stretcher to the Balcombe railway hotel and placed in its stables. A local doctor, Thomas Byass, was called and told that an elderly man had probably strayed over the line and been run over.

Although the man's clothes were soaked in blood, they weren't torn. But the face was badly mutilated, with gashes extending almost from ear to ear and encrusted with congealed blood. In places it was cut right down to the bone. There were also several cuts on the front of the thighs and the body was full of bruises and scratches. Byass soon realised that some of the injuries could have only been caused by a sharp instrument. This was no accident: the man had been brutally murdered.

That evening, the officials examining the compartment found two bullets embedded in the back of one of the seats and another one very close to the communications cord. Lying on the floor was a folded newspaper, the *Family Herald*, and a handkerchief. Both were soaked in blood. Apart from the blood spattered around the compartment there were bloody finger-prints on the footboard which ran along the outside of the carriage and also on the external handle of the door. When the examination was over an order went out to railway staff to look for trespassers or anything suspicious along the line.

Later, a report came in from London Bridge of a man acting suspiciously on a Brighton train which had left an hour after Lefroy's departure. A passenger told an official there that when the train stopped at Three Bridges a 'rough looking man' in shabby clothes and smelling of drink had entered his compartment. He appeared nervous and excited and was covered with mud from head to foot, as if he had rolled down an embankment. His umbrella was also covered in mud. The passenger thought it was strange, particularly as the day had been so hot and dry. The man started to light a pipe but put it out when the passenger told him it was a non-smoking compartment.

The man carried in his hand a small white cardboard box, wrapped in brown paper and fastened with string. During the journey he untied the string, took the brown paper off, carefully crumpled it up, opened the carriage window and threw it well clear of the line. After he left the train, the passenger gave the official his description, which was forwarded to the police and circulated immediately. He was about 5ft 8in tall with a very red and thin face. He had short fair hair, a slight moustache and wore a dark suit and a round hat.

On the return journey to London, Lefroy seemed relaxed and chatted to Detective-Sergeant George Holmes about the day's events. Holmes, a muscular solid looking man, asked him if he ever carried a firearm. Lefroy replied that he liked to 'keep a great distance from those things'. When the train stopped at Balcombe, the stationmaster at Three Bridges, Mr Brown, entered their compartment. He whispered to Holmes that a body had been found on the track and that it was best to keep an eye on the injured man. At another stop Holmes' colleague, Howland, left the train and returned to Brighton.

When they reached Croydon station, Lefroy suggested taking a cab to his house as he did not want to be seen in public 'in such a wretched condition'. Just before they left, Holmes was handed a police telegram by the station clerk. He read it quickly and put it in his pocket. After a short journey through rolling hills and green fields the cab stopped at a semi-detached house on the outskirts of Wallington. On the wall outside a brass plaque announced 'An Establishment for Young Ladies'. They had arrived at No. 4 Cathcart Road.

The front door was opened by an elderly nurse who told Lefroy that his cousin, Mrs Clayton, who was expecting a baby, was ill in bed. Lefroy politely invited Holmes into the drawing room and offered to help him with the investigation in any way he could. Mr Clayton appeared. He was shocked at Lefroy's appearance and listened to his account of the assault. Holmes wrote down the details in his notepad. The detective asked Lefroy where he could be contacted tomorrow.

'Wallington, up to twelve. After that at the United Arts Club, Savoy Street, Strand,' he replied.

Holmes asked if he knew the number of his watch. He said it was 56,312. The detective wrote it down and asked if he could check. Lefroy handed the watch over. Holmes fumbled with the back but it wouldn't open. He gave it to Mr Clayton. He couldn't open it either. Eventually, Holmes managed to prise it open.

'You 'ave made a mistake, sir,' he told Lefroy. 'It's 16,261.'

'Yes, I forgot.'

Holmes struck out 56,312 and put in 16,261.

He asked if Lefroy knew the maker's name.

'No,' came the answer,' 'I bought the watch from a friend.'

The interview over, Lefroy accompanied him to the door and thanked him politely for his help, adding that his cousin would probably offer a reward. Holmes assured him Scotland Yard would be informed and that the culprit was sure to be apprehended.

The detective walked slowly back to Wallington Station. He was very tired and longed to get back to his home in Southwark, but he was in for an unpleasant surprise. At the station he was passed another telegram: *From Inspector Howland. Keep the man Lefroy in safe custody until I arrive. By no means lose sight of him.*

Holmes rushed back to Cathcart Road, but he decided to wait for reinforcements instead of entering the house. Almost an hour later, Howland and three policeman arrived and told Holmes to watch the back entrance. Howland knocked on the front door. Mr Clayton opened it. He told him Lefroy had gone to see a local doctor about his injuries. A policeman was sent to check. Lefroy had not been there. The police searched his bedroom on the top floor and found some blood-stained clothes and bandages still wet with blood. Then they waited outside in the darkness for him to return.

From time to time they met curious neighbours who wanted to know what was going on. By the morning it was clear that Lefroy had disappeared. But his surname was not Lefroy: he was, in fact, the son of Staff Commander Henry Mapleton.

The spot where the body was found. [*London Illustrated News*]

3

By late afternoon the next day, as the railway carriage, blinded and guarded, was taken up the line to Balcombe for the inquest, the following police notice began to appear in public places:

WANTED FOR MURDER!

Percy Lefroy Mapleton, alias Lefroy – a reporter aged 22. Height 5ft 8in, thin dark hair cut short, small dark whiskers; last seen at Wallington at half-past nine on the 27th (last night) with his head bandaged. He was dressed in a dark coat and wore a low black hat; had scratches upon his throat, and was wounded, it is supposed by a pistol shot. He had a gold, open-faced watch, No. 16261, maker Griffiths of Mile End Road.

In the evening a conference was held at London Bridge Station and all the staff on duty the day before were questioned by detectives. The driver and fireman on the train claimed that amid the roar of escaping steam and the clanging of the shovel against the sliding coal they had been deaf to everything except the noise of their immediate environment. The guard, Thomas Watson, confirmed that there were no more than 20 passengers on board and that he had not heard any gunshots or fog signals. At East Croydon, he had seen the victim – whom he knew – sitting alone in the carriage. He appeared to be asleep with a white pocket handkerchief thrown lightly over his head. Watson admitted that ' anybody might have got into his carriage without me noticing it'.

One passenger had heard three or four 'explosions' just before the train had entered the Merstham Tunnel. They had upset his small son, already apprehensive about the darkness of the tunnel. The father had told him, 'don't be frightened; they're only fog signals' – an odd assumption considering that the day was clear and bright.

The immediate public reaction was one of concern over the apparent failure of the communicator cord – which alerted the driver – to have saved the man from his fate. The *Daily Telegraph* lamented that:

One of the most terrible circumstances about this tragedy is that a quiet elderly gentleman was being cruelly stabbed to death in a smoking carriage while on the other side of a thin partition several other passengers were, in all probability, reading their papers or dozing or chatting, in total unconsciousness of the fact that they were next door neighbours to murder.

Unsurprisingly, the behaviour of the police and the railway officials involved drew a lot of public criticism and ridicule.

> If the police at Brighton had been confederates of Lefroy, they could not have acted in a more obliging manner. It was a trial of wit between the guardians and the breaker of the law, and the breaker won an easy triumph.
>
> (*Brighton Evening Argus*)

In particular, Detective Sergeant George Holmes and the chief constable of Brighton, James Terry, bore the brunt of the criticism. The *St James Gazette* described Holmes as 'a simple goose of a policeman waiting at the door like a mute'.

While the police were conducting a frantic nationwide search for Lefroy – the name by which he became forever known – the funeral of the dead man took place on an oppressively hot day in Brighton. Most shops shut as a mark of respect, and the whole of the two-mile route from his home to the cemetery was lined with thousands of spectators eager to witness the last journey of the victim of what the press were describing as 'the murder of the century'. Hats were removed as the cortege, consisting of a hearse and four mourning coaches, passed by.

The cemetery itself was full. Those who were unable to gain admission waited outside with a number of street vendors who were busily selling memorial cards. In front of the cemetery gates two singers performed in doleful unison, to the accompaniment of an erratic concertina, a ballad telling the tragic story in doggerel rhymes.

A large crowd watched as the coffin, covered by a black cloth, was removed from the hearse. After a simple service it was brought out of the chapel and laid at the side of the grave which was surrounded by people from all walks of life, the scarlet uniforms of the soldiers being strikingly noticeable. Loaded with floral wreaths and a big bouquet of white roses – placed upon it at the last moment by a niece – the coffin was lowered slowly into the grave. A large brass plate on the centre of the polished elm box bore the following inscription:

FREDERICK ISAAC
GOLD
Died 27th June,
1881,
Aged 64 years.

At the end of the service, the mourners each took a last glance into the grave, after which they returned to their coaches and left the cemetery. When they had gone, many hundreds of bystanders flocked to the grave to look in, but the coffin was almost completely covered from view by flowers.

One mourner had been too upset to attend the funeral – Mr Gold's wife, Lydia. She had been in a state of shock since reading the numbing words of the telegram that had been delivered to her house at 10 pm on 27th June: *Man found dead this afternoon. Name on papers Frederick Gold. He is lying here now. Reply quick – Stationmaster, Balcombe.*

She had expected her husband to arrive home at tea time. By eight she had been so worried she had walked the hundred yards from her house to Preston Park Station and asked the stationmaster if there had been any incidents. Surprisingly, he said there had been none.

Later, after receiving the telegram, she had put on a black veil and had gone to Balcombe with a family friend. On her arrival at the village station she was advised by the police not to see the body lying in the stables. Instead, her friend went and confirmed that it was her husband. Though distraught, Mrs Gold had managed to remember the make and number of the gold watch which had been wrenched from his body.

A few days later she told the inquest, held at the old schoolhouse in Balcombe, that her husband, by dint of hard work, had built up a chain of bakery shops in London before retiring down to Brighton several years ago. They had previously lived in the East End of London where he had become a pillar of the community: a churchwarden, a guardian and an overseer of the poor. The day he died she knew that he was going to London to collect money from the one shop he still owned, but he never discussed financial matters with her. She said he was rather 'close' in money matters. In fact, he hated people enquiring into his affairs. When travelling by train he preferred to find an empty compartment. He would take off his hat and put on a skullcap. If anyone entered his compartment he would pretend to be asleep. She confirmed that he never carried firearms.

A London pathologist found a bullet wound in Mr Gold's neck which had probably only stunned him and believed he had been slashed 14 times with a knife. It was thought that he was still alive when he had been hurled out of the train in the middle of the tunnel. The fall had probably killed him.

The inquest at Balcombe ended with a verdict of wilful murder against Percy Lefroy Mapleton, alias Lefroy. A mass of circumstantial evidence against him had built up in the days following the murder, not least the

Frederick Gold.

fact that the ticket collector Gibson confirmed that Lefroy's blood-stained ticket had been a first class single. But, although the *Times* described the verdict as a 'foregone conclusion', there were some doubts. According to his family Lefroy was a weak man and at least four stone lighter than Gold who, in his wife's opinion, was very strong for his age. Could Lefroy have overcome him in a struggle estimated to have lasted at least 15 minutes? Or did he have an accomplice? Perhaps the passenger who had acted so strangely on the evening of the murder? Mrs Gold had also testified that five years ago her husband had fallen out with his younger brother, Thomas – who used to manage some of the shops – over money matters. Was he somehow involved? The police were still trying to contact him.

During the inquest Mrs Gold identified several items found on her husband or near his body, but she was puzzled that a possession he always carried with him had not been found – his favourite umbrella with her special darning. Where was it? But, with well over a week having passed since the murder, the public were asking a different question: Where was Lefroy?

4

After Lefroy had disappeared, the police made a succession of visits to the home of his cousin, Mrs Clayton, in Wallington. In her words, 'they turned it inside out', ripping up the floorboards and digging up the garden. They were looking for Mr Gold's watch but failed to find it. And, despite a thorough search along the London to Brighton railway line, they had been unable to find any murder weapons either.

The police, though, did establish that early on the morning after the murder Lefroy had visited his younger sister, Julia, at a hospital in Islington where she worked as a matron. He had stayed only a few minutes and had borrowed 14s from her. Then the trail had gone dead.

The police concentrated their search on the capital's workhouses and cheap lodging-houses, for they were fairly certain that he was still in London. The hospitals were also checked, as the doctor who had treated him in Brighton believed he still might need medical attention. Scotland Yard were confident of an early arrest. But three days passed with no success and so in conjunction with the railway company they offered a reward of £200 for his apprehension.

Next day, Friday 1st July, newspaper history was made when, for the first time, the *Daily Telegraph* printed a drawn portrait of a wanted man. Lefroy's 'face' thus became circulated throughout the land. Unfortunately it was inaccurate, and soon more than 50 people who had nothing to do with the crime were arrested. The wanted man was frequently spotted in Wallington and Brighton and at railway stations all the way from the south coast to Scotland. Sometimes passengers pulled the communication cord and refused to travel further with anyone who remotely resembled Lefroy. On one occasion, four 'Lefroys' were arrested on the same day.

The *Brighton Evening Argus* (2/7/1881) illustrated the atmosphere:

At 8.30pm, on Saturday evening, Queen's Road, Brighton, was the scene of great excitement. A tradesman noticed a man whom he believed to be Lefroy walking down the road, and he accordingly followed him. The man turned into North Street where a policeman was met with, and the tradesman charged the officer to take him into custody. The policeman looked at him and said he was not the man. He therefore refused to take him into custody, and upon this the tradesman said if he let him go he would do so at his own peril. By this time a large crowd had collected, and great excitement prevailed. Several persons cried out, 'There is the murderer, there is the man who killed Mr Gold'. And the conduct of the mob was such a character that the constable deemed it advisable to convey the man to the town hall in order to protect him from its violence.

Some hundred of people followed the constable and the man to the police station, where he was immediately recognized by the

MURDER,
£200 · REWARD.

WHEREAS, on Monday, June 27th, ISAAC FREDERICK GOULD was murdered on the London Brighton and South Coast Railway, between Three Bridges and Balcombe, in East Sussex.

AND WHEREAS a Verdict of WILFUL MURDER has been returned by a Coroner's Jury against

PERCY LEFROY MAPLETON,

whose Portrait and Handwriting are given hereon,—

and who is described as being 22 years of age height 5 ft 8 or 9 in., very thin, hair (cut short) dark, small dark whiskers ; dress, dark frock coat, and shoes, and supposed low black hat (worn at back of head), had scratches from fingers on throat, several wounds on her t, the dressing of which involved the cutting of hair, recently lodged at 4, Cathcart Road, Wallington, was seen at 9.30 a.m. 26th ult., with his head bandaged, at the Fever Hospital, Liverpool Road, Islington. Had a gold open-faced watch (which he is likely to pledge). " Maker. Griffiths, Mile End Road, No 16261."

One Half of the above Reward will be paid by Her Majesty's Government, and One Half by the Directors of the London Brighton and South Coast Railway to any person (other than a person belonging to a Police Force in the United Kingdom) who shall give such information as shall lead to the discovery and apprehension of the said PERCY LEFROY MAPLETON, or others, the Murderer, or Murderers, upon his or their conviction ; and the Secretary of State for the Home Department will advise the grant of Her Majesty's gracious PARDON to any accomplice, not being the person who actually committed the Murder, who shall give such evidence as shall lead to a like result.

Information to be given to the Chief Constable of East Sussex, Lewes, at any Police Station, or to

The Director of Criminal Investigations, Gt. Scotland Yard.

JULY 4th, 1881.

(4313)   Harrison and Sons, Printers in Ordinary to Her Majesty, St. Martin's Lane.

A widely circulated wanted poster.

officer on duty as a workman employed at the railway station. After a few moments the suspect was allowed to leave the town hall by the side door, but for more than an hour afterwards a large crowd remained near the gates of the market, anxious to catch a glimpse of Lefroy, whom it was believed had been captured.

One man was arrested so many times that the police gave him a printed form of passport to stop him being re-arrested. Another, an American tourist, begged the police to let him stay in their cells for a few days to give him a break from being chased down streets because he looked like Lefroy. According to the *Brighton Guardian*, 'You only have to stand at the corner of a street, scowl viciously for a moment or two, turn up the collar of your coat, and then walk off rapidly, then you are arrested.'

On 7th July, a man in Hereford was charged on his own confession, with being Lefroy's accomplice. But it was shown that he had made the confession while drunk. And an Austrian student shot at people in a London park, shouting 'I am Lefroy' before being taken away by

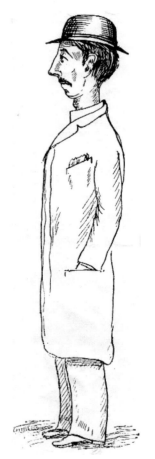

A portrait of Lefroy drawn from memory by a man who knew him, which appeared in his local paper, the *Croydon Advertiser*.

police. He was released when it was realised that he too was drunk.

As temperatures that first week in July soared into the nineties the search for Lefroy became ever more desperate. The police decided to send a circular – authorising house to house searches – to every police station in the country, and two detectives were even sent to the continent. Questions were raised in the House of Commons about only the second murder ever on the national railways, and Sir William Harcourt, the Liberal home secretary, was heavily criticised for the conduct of the investigation. But then the police got a break.

At about 7pm on 8th July – eleven days after the murder – police inspectors Jarvis and Swanson were sitting in their office at Great Scotland Yard when they were informed by a constable that two young men were waiting outside. They said they thought they knew where Lefroy was. The inspectors agreed to see them. When the two men had gone, the detectives and a constable headed for a forgotten area of London, an area where crime and poverty were common bedfellows, an area where even the police themselves feared to tread: the East End.

Jarvis and Swanson stopped their cab in Smith Street, a row of neat working men's terrace dwellings in the heart of the East End, just off the Mile End Road. They leapt out and positioned themselves in the entrance of a church across the road from No. 32. They waited, fixing their eyes on the ornamental ironworks protecting the windows.

The evening was hot, clear and beautiful, and even the squalid surroundings of East London glistened as the roofs and chimney pots caught a shimmer of gold from the setting sun. The detectives listened to the laughter and shouts of children coming from the nearby alleys and streets. They watched working men, tired after their day's labour, sitting at the doors of their houses in their shirt sleeves smoking pipes. Nearby, poorly dressed women with white-faced babies in their arms, gossiped with each other.

After a while, Swanson noticed a young woman go to the arched doorway and open the front door. They quickly followed her in. In the hallway they met a middle-aged woman who introduced herself as the landlady, Mrs Bickers. They showed their identity cards and Swanson suggested they speak in the parlour. He asked her if she had any lodgers:

'Yes, several,' she replied.

'Anybody of the name of Clarke here?'

'Yes, he's an engraver from Liverpool.'

'Which room does he occupy?'

'First floor front.'

'Is he in?'

'Oh yes, he never goes out.'

Swanson informed her about their suspicions and instructed her to wait downstairs. Leaving Jarvis at the rear of the house and the constable at the front, Swanson bolted straight upstairs. He knocked on the door. A strained voice came from within.

'What do you want?'

Swanson, putting on a formal voice answered:'Sorry to disturb you sir; I am looking at the house with a view to purchasing it. May I come in?'

'Be my guest,' came the swift reply.

Swanson slowly opened the door. The room was dark. Adjusting his eyes, he saw, through the thin streams of light that came through the drawn blinds, a shirt sleeved man sitting in an armchair in the corner.

'Percy Lefroy Mapleton . . . ?'

5

'Yes, I expected you.'
The man made no attempt to move. Swanson strode over and handcuffed him.

'Mapleton, I'm a police officer and I'm charging you with the wilful murder of Mr Gold on the Brighton railway on 27th June.'

'I am not obliged,' Lefroy said haughtily, 'to make any reply, and I think it better not to make any answer.'

Swanson formally cautioned him and opened the blinds. Shielding his eyes from the light, Lefroy added, 'I want to qualify my statement by saying I am not guilty.'

Swanson signalled to Jarvis to come up and search the prisoner. Lefroy emptied his pockets. He had only a box of matches and one shilling on him. Jarvis searched the room. He tried to open a chest of drawers but it was locked. Lefroy said he did not have the key so Jarvis went to borrow a chisel from the landlady waiting downstairs.

Swanson studied the man still seated in the armchair. He looked worn out but had no sign of any wound. Swanson's eyes strayed to a medicine bottle on the chest of drawers. It was labelled 'Arnica', a remedy for bruises. He picked up another object and turned to Lefroy.

'Do these scissors belong to you, Mapleton?'

'Yes, I used them for cutting off my moustache and whiskers.'

Lefroy denied knowing anything about a gold watch or revolver. On opening the chest Jarvis found a collar and waistcoat covered in blood, a false moustache and beard, and part of a flannel shirt. He placed them in a black bag.

The detectives led Lefroy down the stairs and ordered a cab. While they waited, Mrs Bickers spoke to her lodger:

'You know, Mr Clarke, that I am innocent of anything that has occurred.'

'Oh, you know nothing about it,' replied the handcuffed man.

She continued, 'I would not have waited upon you had I known you were a murderer, nor would I have had you in my house.'

Lefroy lowered his eyes and said nothing. When the cab arrived, the detectives, with Lefroy between them, pushed their way through a small group of inquisitive neighbours. Once in the cab Lefroy turned to Jarvis.

'I am glad you found me, I am sick of it. I would have given myself up in a day or two. I have regretted it ever since I ran away. It put a different complexion on the case, but I could not bear the exposure. I feared certain matters in connection with my family would be published. I suppose I shall be allowed to see a lawyer?'

Jarvis nodded his head.

By the time they arrived at Scotland Yard a large crowd had already begun to assemble outside. From there, Lefroy was taken to Westminster police station. He complained that he hadn't eaten all day and was provided with coffee and sandwiches. After eating, he lay down on a plank bed, and, still fully dressed, put his head to the wall and fell asleep.

Back at Mrs Bicker's house, the police were threatening to book a number of cab-drivers with sightseers who were blocking the road and causing an obstruction. By midnight, the street was full of people. Besieged by inquirers, Mrs Bickers sought the aid of a friend who stood with his back to the front door and, shaking his head sagely at every argument, refused to let anyone enter.

Early next morning the gates of the police station were thrown open. Cries of 'Here he comes!' and 'Here he is!' were raised as a gathering of several hundred people pushed, jostled and shouted around an outgoing cab. The driver quickly whipped his horse into a brisk gallop as policemen came running out of the station and pushed the mob away from the cab doors and windows. Soon the crowd was left behind and the vehicle made its way unnoticed down Victoria Street to Victoria Railway Station. Inside sat the pale figure of Lefroy and three detectives.

At the main terminal there was a much bigger crowd containing a large number of railway employees on their breakfast break. As Lefroy was escorted along the platform for Brighton, yells and hisses were hurled at him and the crowd stampeded and made a great rush to get a sight of him. They were forcibly held back by a strong body of police as the unmanacled man was put into a First Class compartment. Once seated, the detectives quickly pulled down the blinds.

It was perfect holiday weather. A light wind chased some clouds along the sky and blew the engine's smoke across the railway yard as the train departed. At every station, crowds gathered to catch a glimpse of Lefroy but were thwarted by the blinds. The embankments too were lined with people wildly cheering the train as it sped by.

At Haywards Heath Lefroy had to change trains. As he walked along the platform carrying a bundle of blood-stained clothes, the passengers remaining on the train gave him a torrent of abuse. Looking very dejected with his head hung down, he was quickly taken to the Lewes train standing in a siding. A reporter from the *Daily Telegraph* (11/7/1881) recorded the scene:

I saw a miserable youth sitting back in the compartment, trying to cover his face with his hands, and breathing heavily, seemed to suffer terribly. One of the side blinds of the new carriage would not draw to the bottom and so it was easy to see in. Like a peep show ladies and gentlemen took it in turns to look . . . a father lifted up his pretty golden-haired little girl, and as he put her tenderly down, she clapped. Thus for nearly an hour the platform was kept as a promenade of sightseers, speaking their minds freely about Lefroy within hearing of that wretched man, so that, looking from the crouching, frightened figure inside to the good-humoured, excited, and manifestly delighted mob on the other side of the carriage door, I could hardly help wondering at the seeming absence of compassion, even among the women, who appeared to laugh loudest.

At Lewes, a prison van waiting in the forecourt of the station whisked him away to the prison. It was followed all the way by a large mob shouting 'hang him' and 'tear him to pieces'. At the prison gates he was handed over to the deputy governor. After a cold bath and a medical examination he was marched down passages and through several iron gates, holding onto his trousers as his belt had been confiscated. He was placed in a small, dimly lit whitewashed cell with barred windows of grooved glass at one end and a black door at the other. It was furnished with a tiny, roughly made up one-legged table fixed to wall, a chair, a bucket with a lid, a jug of water and a ceramic basin.

Lefroy was informed by the governor that he could be supplied with any extra food which he or his 'friends' might be able to pay for. He spent the day reading the books provided for him in his cell. He apparently slept well his first night, closely watched by an extra warder who kept an eye on him through the spyhole with its moveable metal shield in the door.

The following day, he was seen by detectives and told them the murder had been committed by the third man in the train compartment. He also saw his solicitor, Mr Dutton, and strongly maintained his innocence, promising to reveal startling new evidence which would throw a different light on his conduct. The first person he wrote to in prison was his cousin, Mrs Clayton:

My darling Annie,

The particulars of my coming here are of course only too well known to you, and I need not pain either you or myself by mentioning them again. God will, I firmly believe, yet extricate me from this terrible position, and that is the one thought that keeps me up . . . Dearest, you, in spite of all my faults, know me better than to believe me capable of taking the blood of a poor old man.

Love Percy.

6

Percy Lefroy Mapleton was born in Peckham, London on 23rd February 1860. It is probable that his father, Staff Commander Henry Mapleton, gave him his middle name in honour of a man who he knew well while stationed at St Helena, Lieutenant General Sir John Henry Lefroy. Sir John later established his reputation as a geographer and eminent meteorologist in Canada where a peak in the Rocky Mountains, Mount Lefroy, was named after him.

At the time of his birth Lefroy's father was 45 years old and still at sea. His mother, Mary Trent Seale, was the daughter of a major in the English army who owned an estate in St Helena. Lefroy's family was undoubtedly quite well off, and the Mapletons in particular had a 'good pedigree' with one of their forbears being Jane Austen's doctor.

Lefroy's early years were spent living with his mother, his two sisters Mary and Julia – 15 and 13 years older respectively – and his uncle and aunt, Captain and Mrs Archibald Seale and their two children Frank and Annie (later to become Mrs Clayton). Lefroy later reported that at birth his mother 'was in extremely delicate health, being in a rapid decline and also suffering from palpitations of the heart. But under all agonies she was perfectly resigned, never complaining, never reproachful, and unspeakably grateful for the smallest kindness bestowed upon her or those she loved . . . I can sincerely say she was beloved by all who had the good fortune to know her.'

She died when he was just six years old, and the deaths of a grandmother and one of his favourite uncles followed in the same year:

'I was too young to realize the awful loss properly then,' he wrote, 'but have often done so long since. I remember I mourned for them as deeply as my young buoyant heart would permit; more especially for my uncle who was cut down by heart disease within half an hour of returning from church.'

Lefroy was brought up by his aunt. His father was, in his own words 'very far from what a father and husband should have been'. He showed little interest in his son and never really lived with him. At his wife's death he was living with his daughters on a half pension and apparently drinking heavily and draining the family's resources. He had had an interesting career – apart from his voyages he had witnessed the exhumation of Napoleon's body on St Helena and its return to France – but he had never attained the success he had aspired to.

A family friend later remembered that when Lefroy was a child 'he was a pale, puny lad, receiving his education at home, and inclined to be reserved and self-contained on all occasions. From his birth he has been so sickly and delicate that no one ever expected him to live . . . Later, in addition to the extreme feebleness of his frame, his characteristics were almost foolish generosity and gentleness, but ever coupled with eccentricity of the most pronounced type.'

When he was seven, Lefroy was sent to a school for 'young gentlemen' and learned to read and write well. Then he was sent to the 'little boy's department' of a school which his cousin, Anne Clayton, had opened for young ladies. Two of his classmates were grandsons of the famous Josiah Wedgewood. In school Lefroy was the perfect boy, studious, attentive and obedient. But at home he was different: 'I was still the quiet nervous child of strong imagination but . . . I was beginning to lie in very childish ways but still lie. Owing to my delicate health I was not corrected as a more robust child might have been.'

Two happy years passed, for even the severe and dangerous attacks of bronchitis which occurred in them he did not regard in any way as bars to being happy. Rather the reverse, in fact, for when he was ill everything was done by his devoted relatives to make him happy. At the age of 10 he was sent to a large grammar school, St Mary's college in Peckham, but he did not remain there long. The boys there were 'too rough' for a delicate child, so he was sent to the Royal Navy school at New Cross. Although he complained that it was an indisciplined school, in the 18 months he spent there he won many prizes. During this time his father never came to see him or even wrote. Instead, Lefroy developed a particularly close relationship with his cousin, Frank Seale, who was 20 years older.

'At this period,' he wrote, 'I used to regularly go to Church with my dear cousin Francis Seale, and those Sunday walks to church with him form one of the happiest memories of my young life. He was so kind and loving to me. Ever ready to tell me the meaning of this or that or do anything for me, and never shrinking from reproving me gently when I deserved it. He was always like a loving older brother to me.'

Lefroy also began to show a genuine interest in the theatre. His aunt, however, because of her High Church morals, looked upon theatres and actors as temples and followers of the Devil, and she barred him and her own children from any contact with them. By the time he was 14 he was 'very thin, very pale and tall' for his age and still a rather sickly youth. He had become very studious, perhaps because physical exertions were barred to him, and had developed a love of writing. In fact, his father, had also liked to write and when he was working had contributed factual and descriptive articles about his voyages to the *Nautical Magazine*.

However, Lefroy's old habit of deceiving was now even stronger than before, for his 'wonderfully fertile imagination' fostered this habit immensely. It had got to the stage where 'telling a lie seemed just as easy as telling the truth'. Despite this, he considered his nature was as loving and gentle as of old. He finished his education in a large private school in Peckham and made the greatest possible progress, winning prizes for Latin, French, English and mathematics. In August 1876, he left school with the 'rudiments of a good education, undecided in character, delicate in health, tossed on the stormy sea of doubt as to what was right or wrong. No kindly father's hand to guide me, launched on the treacherous ocean of the world.'

After school, according to his family, Lefroy showed an interest in becoming a lawyer and studied furiously to that end but failed to get on a course. He also started to get involved in petty deceptions. Eighteen months later we have a glimpse of his state of mind in a letter he wrote to his cousin, Anne Clayton, whilst he was on holiday on the Isle of Wight:

Ventnor, March 29 1878.
Dear Annie,
You are quite correct when you say I am 'more cheerful'. This is the reason, when I first came here, perhaps you may remember that I knew <u>no one</u>. After Christmas I made many acquaintances and I hope a few friends. Of course most of them were young fellows of the ages from 18 to 25. There were of course many <u>good</u> and some I am sorry to say, the reverse. Among the latter set, I should have assuredly fallen, but for the timely advice given me by someone, who was a comparative stranger to me. Four times I was saved from commencing that dreadful course, alas, so familiar to <u>T. James</u>. But whenever I was tempted by the Devil; those few honest words of advice, coupled with a kindly face I never shall forget, brought before me the enormity of the sin I was about to commit and made me throw aside the horrible thoughts in disgust.

My last temptation was on 28th February. On that date I had an appointment to keep in the evening at 7.30. All day, God only knows how I prayed and struggled to do the right, but seemingly without avail. At last I made up for the wrong. All the bad arguments had triumphed only too easily. At a few minutes to the appointed time I walked out of the house, and paused for an instant to look at the lovely sunset. At that minute there was a sudden gust of wind which blew the dust into my eyes. I drew out my handkerchief and something fell to the ground at my feet. I picked it up. It was something which had been given me by the person I have mentioned before. Like lightning I saw my <u>real</u> position. That earnest voice rang in my ears, and those clear truthful eyes seemed to look me full in the face, as I stood there in the twilight irresolute. But the right conquered at last, and I was saved. Since then I feel as firm in that way, as I am in total abstinence, though very often when committing smaller sins, one look at my little keepsake and I feel altogether strengthened. That night I made a solemn vow to show my gratitude to the person I have named. Can you wonder that I feel grateful? All this happened before I came up last time. Since then I have had a terrible nightmare. From it, I am <u>sure</u> my benefactor is in <u>deadly</u> peril, perhaps of life and I am so firmly convinced that I shall be enabled to defeat the project, and then wipe out a little of the debt I owe. I sincerely hope Julia will not come here, as I am not at all up to the mark. Last Wednesday, I was reading, and just happened to look up, when in a minute I saw <u>it</u> and fainted dead away. I hope dear you will excuse these wretched letters but you must put it down to my not having more <u>out</u> than <u>in</u> my senses for three weeks. I will do as you wish concerning the Wedgewoods. I intend to go there on Monday.

With fondest love,
Your affectionate Cousin, Percy.

It is a disturbing letter, showing a tortured soul trying to overcome temptation and possibly suffering from delusions. It also indicates that he was on rather a long holiday; perhaps an attempt by his family to remove him from trouble he was getting into at home. But it was only a temporary solution, for in September of that year an actor, Mr F. Scudamore, sent the following letter to the popular theatrical magazine, the *Era*:

A person professing to have secured the provincial rights of Old Soldiers, Weak Women, Robinson Crusoe, Partners for life etc. wrote and offered liberal terms to several ladies and gentlemen advertising themselves disengaged in the 'Era'. He sent a list of respectable theatres he had secured for this tour. Misled by the list of towns and prices, I accepted his offer and made a joint engagement for myself and my wife for a tour of three months, to open at Ipswich on the 9th inst., in the comedy 'Artful Cards'. When about to start on our journey we received a telegram informing us a delay had occurred and that the tour would not commence till 16th in Gloucester, but half salaries would be allowed.

We arrived at Gloucester in due time. On asking for Mr Percy Mapleton we were told that he had not been seen, that his Acting

Manager had left the town in disgust, and that Mr Mapleton had gone to Paris. One after another the ladies and gentlemen of the company arrived, and each one was told the same comforting story. Some like myself and my wife had come very long journeys in order to keep this engagement, and, I leave actors to judge of our feelings when we discovered that we were the victims of an adventurer, whose object evidently was to engage a strong company, put out an attractive programme, and on Friday night or Saturday morning abscond with the receipts. If it were not a hoax the man could have no other object, but he had not quite money or pluck enough to complete his villainous scheme.

Is this vagabond to escape without punishment? Is there no criminal law that can lay hold of him? He brings people from all parts of the country including Scotland and Dublin. Some, in anticipation of what promised to be a good engagement, have remained idle for a week, thus making a fortnight or three weeks they will lose, in addition to a heavy railway fare. Some ladies engaged have bought new and expensive dresses for the parts they expected to play . . . By kindly inserting this letter in your valuable paper it may be the means of eliciting information which may lead to the punishment of this impostor.

Scudamore learned, too, that no arrangements had been made with the proprietors of the various comedies. It also transpired that the acting manager, engaged by Lefroy through an advert in the *Era*, had tried to meet him but had always been palmed off with excuses. The matter was placed in the hands of a solicitor, but Percy Mapleton had left his address in Nunhead, London, and could not be traced. By October 1878, as many as 60 well known actors and actresses had either been duped or hoaxed by offers of engagements by letters written by 'Percy Mapleton' or 'John Howson'.

It was an audacious scam and seemingly one doomed to failure, for as soon as this young boy of 18 revealed himself to the performers surely his credibility would have been lost. And how could he have managed to put on various plays without the living authors' permission? His reward was small – in this case no reward at all, for he must have spent money on postage and advertising. According to Scudamore, through lack of support from the other actors no summons was brought out against Lefroy for this attempted deception.

Shortly afterwards he received an advance on his mother's inheritance and, kitted out with new clothes, was sent to Australia. His family said it was for health reasons and to obtain a good appointment. It could also have been another attempt to remove their eccentric relative from the trouble he was getting into.

So, by the time Lefroy went to Australia, his unchecked boyhood habit of lying had developed into something far more serious and he was getting into trouble with the law. His posing as a theatrical producer illustrated another facet of his character because, above all, it seems to have been an attempt to be 'somebody', to be important, to escape from the reality of his own life.

7

Lefroy did not sleep very well during his first few nights in prison. Apart from the wooden bed which made him feel sore all over – like being beaten with a stick – he was not yet used to the horrid hush at night broken by prisoners sobbing or the shrieking of someone in a nightmare or to the rapping of mysterious codes on the pipes by which the inmates communicated. All through those long and lonely nights he lay awake until hearing the ugly voice of the prison bell at 6 am which commanded prisoners to get up and dress.

After washing, slopping out and cleaning his cell he ate the breakfast fare of gruel and bread. At 8.30 the shout 'chapel' went up and the prisoners' doors were thrown open. They were formed into a single file - amid a running fire of abuse from the warders – on landings that reeked with the stench of slops and excrement. As they were taken slowly along to the chapel they were forbidden to go near the railings of steel rods or to look at the wire nets dangling between the individual floors placed as if to break the fall of trapeze artists. At the morning services Lefroy could not help noticing the singing of rude songs under the shelter of the surrounding voices; nor the surreptitious nods and winks of the other prisoners.

During the day he occupied himself by writing to his family and friends, requesting food and clothes. He was visited by his solicitor, Mr Duerdin Dutton – who had been hired by his family – and his assistant, Mr Smith. To them, and to the visiting detectives from Scotland Yard, he stuck to the account he had given the Brighton police. He was allowed half an hour exercise each day in the yard and, with talking between prisoners strictly forbidden, spent the time counting the tier upon tier of prison shutters. Each day his racking cough grew worse and worse until on his fifth day he was transferred to a large infirmary cell which he shared with two other prisoners.

As Lefroy waited in prison for the magistrates' enquiry to begin, Mrs Bickers gave the newspapers an account of his stay in Stepney.

'Mr George Clarke' had knocked on her door a little after eleven on the morning of Thursday 30th June. He had seen the 'Lodgings to Let' sign in her window and had agreed to pay 6s a week rent. He gave her a deposit and said he would pay the balance on Sunday. Mr Clarke told her he was an engraver from Liverpool and needed plenty of peace and quiet as he had work to do. Her first impression was that he was a thin, delicate looking man with a quiet demeanour and gentlemanly tone of voice. She could tell he was hard up by his shabby clothes and poor diet of bread and cheese.

After a few days, Mrs Bickers claimed she began to get suspicious about her new lodger. He rarely went out – saying the weather was too hot – and kept his blinds and curtains permanently drawn. Whenever she entered his room he always seemed to be putting his 'tools' away. Moreover, 'Mr Clarke' insisted on having all his meals in his room and refused to have Sunday lunch with the other lodgers, saying he felt too ashamed of his worn clothes to sit with them. Her other tenants told her they had seen him walking in nearby streets smoking a pipe after dusk. They assumed he was probably unemployed.

One day, 'Mr Clarke' told her he was expecting a letter but was worried lest it went astray as he had given the address as No. 33 instead of 32. The day before his arrest it finally arrived. Mrs Bickers took it up to his room. It was locked, so she slid it under the door. He came down later at noon; said he had no money and asked her if she would mind taking a cab into the city to collect his wages. She said she couldn't and asked why he could not go himself. He said he had sprained his ankle getting out of bed.

He decided to send a telegram instead and paid a lad living nearby to take it to a post office. It was addressed to a 'Mr F. Seale' at a small firm in the city. At the post office the boy made a copy and later showed it to Mrs Bickers. It said: *Please bring me my wages this evening, about eight, without fail. Shall have flour in the morning. 32 not 33. From Mr G. Clarke.*

Nobody came that evening with his wages. The next morning the landlady saw him coming downstairs wearing another lodger's coat and immediately went to the local police. She told them she feared he might be a swindler who was about to leave without paying his rent. As he was barely two days in arrears, they advised her not to worry. But she continued to do so and later that day sent her daughter, Clara, to the firm in the city. There, Clara spoke to a young man who informed her that no G. Clarke was employed by them and no telegram had been received for anyone by the name of Seale. And there the matter had rested until the surprise arrival of the Scotland Yard detectives that evening.

Afterwards, one newspaper speculated on Lefroy's mental state while on the run:

Never, perhaps, did a man lead a much more wretched life, who was not actually subjected to torture, than PERCY LEFROY MAPLETON whilst living in Stepney. Universally suspected of a cold-blooded and brutal murder, with the walls around him, which, however crude they might be, did yet give a general notion of his personal appearance, and with but a few shillings in his pocket, Lefroy's existence would have been miserable enough, had there been no other cause of misery. But to all these sources of torment, there was added the horror of thought! If he was guilty, when could the ghastly form of the old man he had murdered cease to be present to his view? In the long watches of the night, how could he escape from the presence of the form which the murderer, be he whom he might, would give all he ever had in the world to bring to life again? And in the long, long day, he had nothing to occupy him but thought, and thought to the murderer means torture. How he must have envied the very poorest and meanest of those East End toilers – hewers of wood and drawers of water – who live in the wilderness of bricks and mortar about Arbour Square, Stepney, which is traversed by the great Commercial Road which leads from Whitechapel to the East and West India Docks. Alas, he can never again be one of the ordinary toilers on earth's surface. He has, if guilty, cut himself off from his kind by one of those deeds of horror of which men start aghast. Half England is thinking of reading of that poor skulking figure of a man who, when the night comes on, ventures for a few brief moments to flit around the only refuge he has on earth, No. 32 Smith Street. Members of Parliament are questioning Ministers respecting him in Parliament, and here he is barely able to maintain existence on a miserable crust of bread and cheese, which he dreads his fellow-lodgers may see and regard contemptuously. The newspapers are full of him; men are being arrested even in the far north on the suspicion that they are he, and he, amidst frightful dreams of his horrible crime, is anxiously speculating on the question, how to get a few shillings to pay his rent.

(*Sussex Agricultural Express* 12/7/1881)

Despite capturing Lefroy, the police were given little credit by most newspapers and satirical magazines. They pointed out that he had been recaptured within an hour's walk from Scotland Yard. More embarrassingly it was reported that a police sergeant living opposite No. 32 Smith Street had actually been spotted on a couple of occasions chatting to Lefroy in a local pub in the evening. Amid the public debate about the value of vaccination there emerged a popular joke:

Why is it unnecessary to vaccinate a policeman?
Because he never catches anything!

Unsurprisingly, *Punch* (16/7/1881) made fun of the force:

The Diary of a Detective

Monday – Got a circular from the Director of the Criminal Investigation Department. He wants me to be 'on the alert'. Always am. Am to keep a sharp look-out for a man with one eye, one arm, and one leg. There's a task for you! Man has got green hair and dark-blue complexion. Have written for further particulars.

Tuesday – Further particulars arrived. The man only speaks a language consisting of one word, 'Jamerangtong', and is dressed as a Chinese Tartar. These details may help me.

Wednesday – I believe I am on the track. Having been told that the man who is wanted smokes a pipe. Saw a person smoking a pipe today. Arrested him, and carried him to the police station. He is believed not to be the man, because he has his full complement of arms, legs and eyes. Moreover, he speaks several languages fluently, has brown hair and a white complexion. Advisable to detain him. The cells being full, we made room by dismissing a prisoner who had been arrested by mistake. The prisoner arrested by mistake had one eye, one arm, one leg, green hair, and a dark blue complexion. He was dressed as a Chinese Tartar, and could speak only a language consisting of one word, 'Jamerangtong'.

Thursday – Prisoner arrested yesterday and kept in the cells all night, not the man. We are rather sorry we allowed the other man to go, as he certainly resembled the kind of person wanted in some particulars. Found that the liberated man had cast his skin on leaving the police station. Shall wear it for a change tomorrow.

Friday – My disguise saves me from Police interference. Have been chasing a man all day. He is always giving me the slip. To secure his confidence I have dyed my hair green, and my complexion dark blue, and have closed one eye, and after tying up a leg and an arm. Surely this should bring him near me now that a reward has been offered. No. Whenever he sees me coming he runs away!

Saturday – At last, when he was not looking, I crept up to him! I rushed at him! I closed with him! And then came my surprise! In self-defence he arrested me! He is a Detective too! We have just heard that a person exactly answering the description of the person wanted is staying at 22 Araminta Villas, East, five minutes walk from where this diary is written. He has paid his bill up to today, Saturday, and has told his landlady that he is going to quit England quietly this evening. He starts at a quarter past eight, and it is now half past seven. We must really look into all this on Monday.

P.S. Some person in no way connected with the police (confound his impudence) has given information at Scotland Yard, and the man is arrested. This is uncalled for officiousness. Why interfering with the police when in the execution of their duty? It is disgusting. What's the good of being a detective if we're not allowed to detect in our own way? Why be in such a hurry?

Mrs Bickers, on the other hand, was hailed as a national hero. Verses were even written in her honour:

THE LAMENT OF THE RAILWAY DETECTIVE

Oh! Please, have you seen the man that we missed,
With his manners so easy and free?
He'd a blow on his head, and a scratch on his wrist;
Oh! Where can that gentleman be?
    (*Chorus of picked Detectives*).
Oh! where; oh! where is our prisoner gone?
Oh! where; oh! where can he be?
With his neck so thin, and his nose so long;
Oh! where can our prisoner be?

Ooray! Ooray! They've got him at last;
They've captured him down at Stepnee,
And his land-lady fair will go in for the bunts,
Thou an artful old gal she must be!
    (*Chorus of exultant Detectives*)
Down there, down there, has our prisoner been,
A hiding away from we,
Till that clever old lady just handed him out,
'Ere's your werry good 'elth, Mrs B.

(*Brighton Guardian* 13/7/1881)

The day after Lefroy's arrest, Mrs Bickers went to Scotland Yard to claim the £200 reward money but, much to her dismay, she learned that it was not her suspicions which had led to the arrest and she was turned down. As the police refused to reveal the names of their informants, suspicion centred on the person Lefroy's mysterious telegram had been addressed to Frank Seale. It was a name already known to the public.

Seale worked as a clerk at the City firm Clara had visited. He was also the 40-year-old second cousin of Lefroy who had caused public indignation at Mr Gold's inquest by his flippant remarks to the coroner. The coroner had, in fact, made him take the oath twice because of his behaviour. Seale shared a bedroom with Lefroy at Mrs Clayton's house. He had shocked the court by saying that he and Lefroy were in the habit of kissing each other every morning and evening and sometimes wore each other's clothes. Seale testified that his cousin occasionally travelled first class, a fact contradicted by Mrs Clayton's husband Thomas, and that Lefroy possessed a gold watch. Rather suspiciously, Seale failed to explain to the coroner why he had arrived home after midnight on the night of the murder.

In the wake of Lefroy's capture, a reporter from the Press Association interviewed Seale. He said he thought the telegram addressed to him was either a hoax – his family had already received many anonymous letters – or that the police had sent it to induce him to visit No. 32 Smith Street. He strongly denied any knowledge of Lefroy's movements or whereabouts while on the run and said he had never heard of 'Mr Clarke'. He believed the phrase 'shall have flour in the morning' was the 'expression of a lunatic'.

At the end of the interview he was asked: 'Had you known that Lefroy was passing as Clarke, what would you have done on the receipt of the telegram?'

'Had I known or had any inkling that the telegram came from Lefroy,' he replied, 'I would have gone to Smith Street at all risks and hazards. I have been very fond of him. He always has been the pet of the family and we are terribly anxious as to his fate. I do not believe Lefroy was *compos mentis*.'

Meanwhile the police were still desperately trying to find Mr Gold's watch and the murder weapons before the magistrates enquiry began. The area between the Merstham tunnel (where the first shots were fired) and the Balcombe tunnel was proving difficult to search. Possessing a long lake and thick woody undergrowth, it meant that anything thrown from a carriage into them might remain undiscovered for a long time.

But the police had discovered a 'vital' witness; a witness they believed would conclusively prove Lefroy's guilt.

8

Lefroy had set off for Australia at the beginning of 1879. It took nearly two months for his boat, the 'Somersetshire', to arrive at the natural harbour of Port Philip in Victoria. He was in a nervous state and later recalled that 'until the vessel was out at sea, I seemed to recognize in every man who looked at me a detective, such is the effect of a guilty mind and not until the white cliffs of old England were mere clouds on the horizon did I breathe a sigh of relief and go down to see that my berth was alright little dreaming that the quiet elderly gentleman who shared my cabin with me was Detective Hockney of the Lincolnshire police in hot pursuit of an absconding bank cashier!'

The journey was uneventful, but Lefroy found it a strange life, 'this sudden severance from a kind home and loving friends to be thrown abruptly among a lot of strangers'. His fellow passengers comprised old colonials returning from an English trip, fortune seekers and adventurers. According to him, for the first time in his life he played cards for money – the favourite pastime on all large passenger ships – and by the end of the voyage had lost £7. He found that 'nearly every passenger where I was, drank, played cards or otherwise profaned the Day of Rest and a better school for unlearning religious principles could not possibly have been found for men'

When he landed he was already depressed, for everyone had told him that 'nothing under £50 was any good' and he only had £35 on him.

Lefroy decided to immediately telegraph home for money saying that he was ill and wanted to return home. He then went and stayed at a hotel in Melbourne. His family had provided him with letters of introduction to the Bishop of Melbourne and to a manager of a national bank, but he made no effort to see them because of his intention of swiftly returning home. Instead, he spent his time enjoying himself: attending lectures, and going to theatres and concerts.

His money soon 'melted like butter in the rays of the sun', and by the time the mailboat arrived six weeks later he had only five pounds left. On its arrival, he rushed down to the post office and was shocked to discover that there were no letters for him. Dismayed at the apparent 'cruel neglect' of his family, he decided to try and economise and last out till the next mail arrived in a month's time. By the time it did he was virtually penniless and had had to sell most of his clothes for about a tenth of their value.

For the second time Lefroy went down to the post office and was handed two letters. The second he read 'turned my heart to stone and made me feel indeed the desperate condition I was in'. For one of his relatives had booked him a return berth on a boat which was not due to depart for another seven weeks. That night he sold the few remaining things he had and paid the rent he owed. He then wandered the city answering advertisements for waiters, shop-assistants and cabmen, but his efforts were fruitless and he was turned out of his lodgings.

'With the Australian winter coming on,' he wrote later, 'I was without a house or home of any sort, only an old coat and shirt on my back . . . penniless, friendless and alone. And for this I believed then that God sent it justly upon me as a punishment for my deceptive conduct and the utterly ungodly life I had led in England.'

The first night of misery he passed on a bench in Prince's Park and the next day looked for any type of menial job. 'Too delicate' was the answer in one place, 'no references' in another, while his racking cough and pallid face told against him in a third. But his sickly condition did procure him a meal on several occasions, as he received small quantities of money from sympathetic passers-by. Australia had no workhouses, so he slept where he could, on benches, under archways or under small boats which lay bottom upwards in boat-yards.

One evening, Lefroy felt so desperate he almost jumped into the river Yarra but something in his head stopped him at the last moment. Afterwards he was discovered wandering about by a friendly policemen who told him to try to get board and lodgings at the Emigrants Home which was a refuge for a small number of destitute immigrants supported entirely by private subscriptions. They accepted him and he remained there until his ship 'True Briton' set sail on 6th July 1879: 'I bid farewell to Australia thoroughly ashamed of myself and deeply repentant for the past.'

The ship completed the 12,000 mile journey in three months. Back in London he made his way to his cousin Anne Clayton's house in Wallington. He was literally in rags and half-starved.

Shortly after his arrest, the *Manchester Guardian* (11/7/1881) published an article by 'one who knew Lefroy' in Australia:

During my stay in Australia, when I was for several years engaged in journalism, I was, on many occasions brought into contact with the now notorious Arthur Lefroy Mapleton, or as he calls himself Arthur Lefroy. He was first pointed out to me in Melbourne by a brother journalist, with a warning – unfortunately only too necessary and common in the colonies with regard to new acquaintances. At that particular time, Mapleton was, according to my information, gaining a precarious living by writing spicy police reports, and doing other obscure work for an obscure Melbourne newspaper. Subsequently, I had the misfortune to be brought into personal contact with Mapleton by his becoming a contributor to the journal on the staff of which I was engaged. His first impression was not unfavourable. His address was winning, when he pleased, and he conversed with an amount of assurance and apparent knowledge well calculated to produce an impression on the unwary. Possessed of a more than ordinary good knowledge of French, he readily made people believe that the somewhat peculiar alias under which he usually passed was his proper name. As this belonged to a family of repute it is unnecessary to mention it. He never concealed the fact that his real name was Mapleton.

He told various stories about his parentage, the favourite one being that his father, who was dead, had been the incumbent of a well-known church in London, and that his mother was a Belgian lady of good family. Another account was that his father had been a partner in an old firm of solicitors in London, in which his place had been taken by his elder brother. When this latter story was told the clergyman would appear as his mother's brother. Colour being given to the statement by the fact that the name he assumed as an alias was the same as that of a once well-known preacher in the south of London. He also had an immense fund of second-hand literary gossip. Thus he had the real names of writers under celebrated 'noms de plume' by heart, talked familiarly of a highly popular novelist as his friend and professed to have a personal acquaintance with many well known authors. Such remarks, which were his stock in trade, when seeking employment on a newspaper, were frequently successful in beguiling country editors in Australia, and sometimes those connected with papers of a higher class. Mapleton managed to obtain employment on one or other of the newspapers in each of the Australian capitals and the various provincial towns which he favoured with his presence. He had chances innumerable, and was more or less notorious in all the capitals, from Brisbane to Adelaide. That he did not succeed was his own fault.

As to Mapleton's general habits, he was what is termed in colonial phrase a bar loafer. 'Public Houses' were practically his home when he was not a strict teetotaller, which it may be said to his credit, he sometimes was for several weeks at a time. For the most part, however, he hung about the various bars, treating others when he had money, either earned by literary work or received from home (which was apparently the case), or being treated in return for his company. It was, in fact, one of his practices to attach himself to some unpublished shearer and shepherd and make what he could out of him, and his stridulous voice was often heard entertaining not very select companions with poetic and dramatic recitations in bar parlours, while he drank at their expense. His figure was familiar on racecourses where small events came off, and there he mingled with the lower class of betting men, making a book with more or less success. He was frequently mixed up with amateur theatre, entertainments, and on one occasion, which is singularly illustrative of his consummate aplomb, I remember well. He had made himself useful to a troupe of amateurs in a provincial town, and they in turn tended to him a benefit, at which Mapleton was to give a recitation. He appeared on the platform in a somewhat rough morning suit, and excused himself to the audience for not appearing in evening costume by stating that his landlord had that morning made a demand on him for board and lodging, to satisfy which he had been obliged to pawn his dress clothes!

From what is known by me of Mapleton I must confess, however, that I feel a certain amount of astonishment he should stand charged with the crime of murder. It is true in the colonies he brought himself on more than one occasion in unpleasant relations with the police on account of some scurrilous pamphlets which he published when out of other literary employment. But he was of weak physique and in many respects the very last man I should have suspected of being guilty of the daring act committed on the Brighton Railway.

Much of what the reporter remembered – two years after meeting Lefroy – must be considered within the context of the great outcry against him which had grown up whilst he was on the run. It was a sensational murder, 'a romance of real life that outstripped anything the fiction writer was capable of conjuring up'. (*Suspicion Aroused* (1893): Dick Donovan).

The temptation for newspapers to feed popular resentment against Lefroy with exaggerated stories about him was obviously great – so much so that his older sister, Mary, after a while, refused to talk to the press any more because of their 'misstatements'.

The 'one who knew Lefroy' shows him in Australia living in a fantasy world of important people and connections. However, his assertion that he drank and gambled a lot is a questionable one, as Lefroy's friends said that he did neither. On his return from Australia, Lefroy learnt that there were two summons out against him – concerning deceptions over pictures – and that his father had died the previous month. He later claimed that the former had disquieted him more than the latter. He kept a low profile for the next few months, living quietly at Anne Clayton's house in Wallington, quite happy to spend his time playing with her children and reading and writing.

The following spring, because of his lack of money, Anne's husband suggested that he apply for the post of clerk to the local committee 'for securing the return of Messrs Stern and Higgins', the local Liberal candidates in the general election. He described it as very thankless work, there being too much of the 'hale-fellow-well-met' sort of thing, but the pay was good (35s a week) and he put up with it and did a good job.

But Lefroy's real ambition was, through writing, to become somehow involved in the world of the theatre or journalism. Bohemian London really flourished in the 1880s, never more so than in the evenings. Theatres were packed every night, with tickets at half-price after 9pm and with final curtains not coming down till gone midnight when 'certain streets of the West End, and notably the Haymarket, were packed with a roystering mob seeing life'. In Fleet Street, the literary Bohemians smoked their short clay pipes in the streets and lounges and tavern bars, fortifying themselves for the night's work with cups of steaming hot brandy and Irish whisky. Or, they hid away in the coffee shops with their high backed wooden partitions for privacy.

This was the world which Lefroy so desperately wanted to enter; to succeed in.

9

Lewes Prison, Friday 15th July 1881.

At 2 a.m., a young coach driver in Lewes was roused out of bed and told that his services were required. Two hours later Mr Slaughter junior was spotted wildly driving his carriage on the cobbled streets through the town centre and up the hill towards the prison. His mission: to take Lefroy and his three escorts to the magistrates' enquiry at Cuckfield.

During the 15-mile journey through picturesque countryside Lefroy smoked a cigar and chatted freely with his escorts about the beautiful summer morning. On arrival at the pretty Sussex village – set in the midst of fields and farmyards – he was taken to the police station. Back in Lewes, crowds, unaware Lefroy had departed, were beginning to assemble at the railway station, expecting to see him leave by train. The police decoy had worked.

At five minutes to ten precisely the prisoner appeared at the police station door, guarded by a dozen constables. He was put into a carriage and driven the short distance to the vine-covered Talbot Hotel in the high street. There was no heckling from the large crowd outside, just excitement and a deathly hush as, with a firm step, Lefroy strode into the building with a constable either side of him. He was wearing a new dark brown tweed suit with a white collar and black scarf. In his hand he carried a white felt summer hat. He looked like a man on holiday. Upon taking his seat – an armchair just behind his solicitor – he looked straight in front of him, occasionally glancing round at the newspaper artists who were already busily engaged in sketching his features.

There he sat, a direct contradiction of every phrenologist and physiognomist - the art of supposedly judging character from facial characteristics - in the world. I can safely say I have seldom seen a more thoughtful, harmless face, with a broad and deep benevolent forehead, quiet, meditative eyes, a cranium that showed none of the supposed characteristics of the murderer. Lefroy Mapleton seemed to be a man in whose presence any old gentleman might safely place his handkerchief over his head and take a nap in a railway carriage.

(*Daily Telegraph* 16/7/1881)

After the charge against him was read out he rose and in a soft voice confirmed that his full name was 'Percy Lefroy Mapleton'. Then he sat down again, and with arms folded, listened intently to the opening words of the prosecuting barrister.

On Monday 27th June, Frederick Gold left his home in Claremont Terrace at five past eight in the morning and walked round the corner to Preston Park Station. He was dressed in a suit of blue serge. He carried his favourite umbrella – with his wife's special darning – over his left arm by its hooked handle. As the forecast was for another hot day he took it more out of habit than necessity. When he arrived at the station, he chatted briefly with the station-master, Albert Hall, who knew him well as a regular season ticket holder.

He entered an empty First Class compartment of the express train to London Bridge which was due to arrive shortly before ten. In London, Gold collected £38 5s 6d from his shop in Walworth, and deposited £38 at the Whitechapel branch of the London and Westminster Bank. He then paid a visit to Park Lane, where he ordered some flour. He was next seen at 1.50pm by a ticket collector, William Franks, at London Bridge Station, walking up and down the platform with his hands behind his back. He looked in at one compartment but turned away when he saw a man with a young boy.

Franks asked Gold, 'Are you going by the two o'clock, sir?' and he replied, 'Yes, my lad, I will get in in a moment'.

As the barrister went on to describe the rest of the events of 27th June, Lefroy's face betrayed no emotion. At the end of the speech the first and, according to the police, their most vital witness, was called. His name was Henry Creek, and he was the manager of a pawnbroker's shop 300 yards from London Bridge Station. The prosecution alleged that on 21st June, six days before the murder, Lefroy had pawned a revolver at Creek's shop for 5s, and that on the morning of the murder he had returned and redeemed it for 5s 6d. The police had found coloured pawn tickets, from the same shop, for other items in Lefroy's bedroom. One newspaper was less than convinced by Creek's performance:

He may be an intelligent person when the value of a sheet or carpet bag is in question, but he didn't shine as a witness. The prosecuting counsel asked 'Do you know the prisoner?' 'I believe I do,' responded the witness. 'Can you see him?' continued the counsel. The prisoner sat directly in front of the pawnbroker, the witness gaped helplessly at a bevy of ladies who were in a far-off corner. 'Well?' said the counsel, 'Why don't you look for him'. By way of reply, the witness glanced at the magisterial bench. 'He's not amongst the magistrates!' Said the counsel. And the witness then turned towards the reporters, almost pouncing upon them wholesale. Still he did not gaze at the prisoner until, having exhausted the whole range of vision, he was obliged to look at the only spot remaining unexplored – namely, the chair immediately in front of him – and then, with a triumphant wave of the hand, he exclaimed 'That's him!'. Had he discovered a planet with eighteen moons and three wings he could not have been more pleased.

(The *Times* 17/7/1881)

Creek was cross-examined by Dutton, Lefroy's solicitor.
'You are not certain this is the man who pawned the pistol?'
'To the best of my belief he is,' replied the witness.
'You won't swear?'
'No.'
'Now Mr Creek, you say that on 27th June, Lefroy redeemed the pistol. What makes you say it was twelve o'clock?'
'From the amount of work the shop had done.'
'Mr Creek, how long have you known the prisoner?'
'I can't say how long I have known him. Sometimes he pawned things in the name of "William Lee" and sometimes he used "James Leigh".'
'Mr Creek, will you swear they are one and the same person.'
'I cannot say I recognised his face on every occasion but did so on that last occasion.'
His cross-examination ended, Creek rather sheepishly left the courtroom. The witnesses who followed him repeated what they had already said at the inquest. So there was a sense of *deja vu* about the proceedings. Even Lefroy appeared bored. A reporter switched his attention to the locals in the public gallery:

Their faces were a 'three volume story', their behaviour was a study. They could only see by either crowding up to the barricade or leaning over each other's shoulders, yet broiling hot as the day was, and almost suffocating as was the odour of pigsties which came in through the half-opened windows, they cheerfully rushed up, ready apparently to die of suffocation rather than lose one twitch of the prisoner's face. 'E's a wisperin,' said one, singularly like Lefroy in appearance. 'His hair is ver rough,' lisped a pretty, delicate girl, as she looked pityingly over the barricade. 'Why don't they 'an'cuff 'im?' asked a man with a red face who looked like a butcher. 'Which is the murderer?' roared out a farmer's boy. Cuckfield was evidently having a great treat, for Lefroy Mapleton was in full view. There was a decrepid old man who could scarcely toddle, and there were lads in their teens, some farm labourers, and, for all I know, the most remarkable people in the district, all as full of excitement at witnessing the spectacle before them, as though each had been the proud possessor of the reward money themselves.

(Daily Telegraph 17/7/1881)

The next important witness was Thomas Watson, the guard on the train. He testified that as the train passed Hassocks Gate – a few miles south of the Balcombe tunnel – it had slowed to about four miles an hour, but he had not seen anyone get off. During Watson's testimony, Lefroy seemed uneasy, scribbled several notes to his solicitor and studied a railway timetable.

As the day declined into the afternoon Lefroy appeared so sleepy that he nearly let the crumpled hat he held in his hand fall to the ground while he dozed. The court adjourned at 5 o'clock. An hour later, he was driven back to Lewes. As he departed, he was watched by a crowd of curious, silent onlookers.

At ten o'clock the next morning, Lefroy was brought into court and looked brighter than he had been on the first day. All the available standing room and seats were taken. Outside, since early morning, a small crowd had gathered in front of the hotel, but the sun's rays as midday approached soon rendered the high street of Cuckfield much too hot to be comfortable, and the crowd melted away, leaving the possession of the street to a colony of pigeons who searched for food among the straw laid down to deaden the noise of passing wheels.

The first witness was a bluff, hearty sort of man who stumbled as he made his way to the stand. Detective Sergeant George Holmes began his evidence by confirming that, before leaving Brighton, he had searched Lefroy at the railway station and found a gold watch with a broken chain in one pocket and some money – about 16s and three Hanoverian sovereigns – in another. Lefroy told Holmes he must have got the coins playing at whist. Holmes added that he had tried to look at some coloured tickets inside Lefroy's wallet but Lefroy had become indignant and snatched it back saying it was private property. (These were the pawn tickets the police had later found in his bedroom.) The magistrates were not impressed.

'Have you ever seen notices at the Brighton Station warning people to beware of gamblers and pickpockets?' one asked.

'Oh, yes, I see them every day,' replied the detective.

'Did it not occur to you that Lefroy might have been one of these gentlemen? You find a watch in his pocket and those coins that card swindlers have on them.'

Holmes looked uncomfortably at the raised platform where the magistrates sat.

'It did not occur to me. By order of Mr Anscombe, the Brighton stationmaster, Lefroy was passed by officials through the barriers to enter the train for the purpose of going home.'

'Did the officials take off their hats when Lefroy passed?' (*Laughter*)

Unperturbed, Holmes looked at his notes and continued.

'No, sir. At Balcombe station, my colleague, Inspector Howland, beckoned to me and told me that a man 'ad been found dead in the tunnel.'

'Did you tell Lefroy or suspect that he was connected?'

'No, sir. If I 'ad any suspicion I would 'ave removed him from the carriage at Balcombe.'

'During the whole of the time you were with Lefroy you said nothing about the finding of a body in the tunnel or the fact that a body had been found without a watch?' asked an exasperated magistrate.

'No, sir. I stayed at Lefroy's house for about 30 minutes, checking the number of the watch which the first telegram I received 'ad asked me to do, and then walked back to Wallington Station where I found another one asking me to detain Lefroy. I returned to the house within six or seven minutes.'

'What did you do then?'

'I kept observation.'

'What!' exploded a magistrate. 'Do you mean to say you didn't go into the house?'

'No, sir.'

'Did you not think it was your duty to apprehend this man?'

'No, sir. Not by myself.'

'Whilst you were with him, did Lefroy have an opportunity of escaping if he had tried?'

'Yes, sir. He 'ad a favourable opportunity to get off the train platform, but I don't suppose he would 'ave got away. He might 'ave attempted it.'

'Suppose he had attempted to get away, what would you have done then?'

'It would 'ave created suspicion on my part.' (*More laughter*)

The magistrates looked at each other in bemusement before motioning Holmes to leave the stand. His assertion that Lefroy must have escaped out the back way was later contradicted by another witness, Mrs Clayton's servant, Joanna Chamberlain, who said she saw Lefroy, with a sticking plaster on his head, go out through the front door. One newspaper cruelly suggested that a more pitiable spectacle than the detective had seldom been seen in a magistrates' court.

Next, it was Chief Constable Terry's turn to feel the mockery of the court. He had a mild and gentle face, an aspect enhanced by his long sideburns. In his smart brown corduroy frock coat he looked anything but an officer of the law.

One magistrate cross-examined him in an ironic tone: 'When you first saw Lefroy, what did you think of him?'

'I thought, when I first read the report, that he had attempted suicide. When I saw him I put some questions to him, and he answered them so coherently that my opinions were altered.'

'Were you told that there was a pool of blood found in the carriage?'

'No, I did not know until the next day.'

'Were you told the train did not stop until it reached Preston Park?'

'I heard them say so.'

'Or that he only had a single ticket?'

'No.'

'At the end of the interview you offered Lefroy assistance?'

'Certainly, sir. The last thing I said was, "Take care of that man". Lefroy must have conveyed in my mind still that there was something wrong about him. I was only with Lefroy for about five minutes. There was nothing in the police clerk's report about him being robbed, or about shots being fired in the carriage, or about the watch and coins. When a charge is brought by the railway police we do not take it out of their hands. They are entirely separate to us. No charge was made, and I promised to render all the assistance I could in the matter.'

'Now, Mr Terry, you seem to have been very kind to this gentleman, and promised to render all the assistance in your power. Has he seen you since?'

Some of the court officials smiled.

'No, sir.'

'Not even to thank you?'

Terry replied in a soft voice, 'No, sir.'(*See appendix for satirical poem about Terry*).

As the afternoon progressed, the whole court was tired and sleepy as the repetitive evidence took its toll. Iced water and eau de cologne were used to brace the court up but made little difference to the atmosphere. One witness, Joseph Starks – the first ticket collector to see Lefroy at Preston Park – appeared so lethargic he had to be asked to stand up.

When the court adjourned Lefroy looked very depressed as he passed through the doorway of the hotel. He was tightly held by the arms by two sturdy policemen who themselves were followed by four officers. A detachment of other officers quickly formed a square around him and he was marched off with military precision to the police station, followed by an excited group of children.

That evening Frank Seale and Thomas Clayton were allowed to visit Lefroy in his cell. He was overjoyed to see them. He asked affectionately after Mrs Clayton and her family. He told them he was well and not despondent. He did not mention the case. His visitors gave him some clean sheets and food and then returned to Wallington.

10

The magistrates' enquiry dragged on for another two and a half days with the majority of the evidence unfavourable to Lefroy. It was revealed that on the morning of the murder, he had defrauded a local Wallington stationer out of a small sum of money. In the deception he had used Hanoverian coins, the same coins Holmes had found on him and similar to those discovered in the train compartment.

Nearly all the railway officials who had contact with Lefroy on June 27th testified that they thought he was a lunatic who had tried to commit suicide. The Brighton stationmaster, Anscombe, thought he was a 'complete madman.' When he had asked him if he had been hurt he had replied, 'I should think I am, considering I have had four or five bullets in my head.' Then Anscombe spoke about the possibility of a 'third man'.

'I've had a good look at the compartment. There were some bloody fingerprints on and under the footboard outside, as though someone had grasped it. If a person was leaving a train in motion and he felt himself falling, it would be a natural thing for him to catch hold of the footboard in that way.'

'Could someone have got from one compartment to another whilst the train was in motion?' asked a magistrate.

'Yes, a person could have got out at one end of the carriage, walked along the footboard, and entered another compartment, but it would be extremely dangerous. Mind you, the windows would have to be open. And probably only an experienced railway man could do so.'

One or two people had written to the newspapers with accounts of people falling from fast trains without injuring themselves. But there had been no trace of the 'strange' passenger who had returned to London from Brighton an hour after Lefroy.

Mrs Nye Chart, who had been on a picnic the day Lefroy had allegedly come to see her, admitted that, although she didn't know him and had never seen him before, she 'very frequently had letters from persons I have never heard from before . . . If I had been at home and the prisoner had called, I should have seen him.'

Lefroy looked uneasy when witnesses gave evidence about Gold's injuries and even more so when his widow, dressed in black, came forward to testify. While she spoke he seemed to hang down his head, occasionally looking sideways, his lower lip nervously twitching. He only looked up when Mrs Gold spoke about her husband's younger brother, Thomas, whom she had not seen for many years and whom she did not appear to like. (The police had finally managed to interview him and had eliminated him from their enquiries). She finished her testimony by describing her husband as 'a very kind-hearted man, affable and pleasant in company and, so far as I knew, liked by everyone with whom he came into contact'.

The police revealed that they had found her husband's umbrella south of the point where his body was discovered. But what was more to the point, it was found south of the only part of the line where the guard, Watson, had said the train had slowed sufficiently enough for someone to jump off without injuring himself.

The last day of the enquiry, Thursday 21st July 1881, was a beautiful summer's day with hardly a cloud in the sky. Not far from Cuckfield, Brighton was awash with a violent eruption of bunting, Venetian masts and Chinese lanterns, for the town was awaiting the visit of the Prince of Wales and his family. At the station the 'royal' platform was carpeted in a crimson cloth; at its end stood a temporarily erected grandstand for the accommodation of the 'favoured ones'. Hanging from the girders in the centre of the platform, at a height of about 10ft from the floor, were rustic pots of plants. Immediately under the station clock were the words 'Welcome to Brighton' in large red letters, shaded grey, and the royal standard waved high above it.

Back at Cuckfield, Lefroy coughed up blood over breakfast and steeled himself to face the large crowd assembled to see him escorted for the last time from the police station to the hotel. The day was taken up with the evidence of Mrs Bickers and the police inspectors who had arrested him. At the end he was asked to respond to the case against him.

He stood up and said quietly: 'I wish to say nothing in answer to the charge.'

He was asked if he wanted to call any witnesses and replied in the negative. The chairman of the magistrates addressed him: 'Percy Lefroy Mapleton, after due deliberation we have come to the unanimous conclusion to send you for trial at the next assize on the capital charge of murder.'

There was silence. Lefroy rose. In a rather haughty manner he turned to the magistrates and said calmly, 'I reserve my defence,' then bowed slightly to the bench before resuming his seat.

Once outside the court he was placed in the centre of a phalanx of 12 policemen and marched off towards the police station. As he passed down the road, long lines of men, women and children watched him in complete silence. He was taken back to Lewes Prison by coach.

Meanwhile, court witnesses, spectators and officials made their way to Haywards Heath Station hoping to catch the Brighton train in time for the Prince's visit. While waiting on the platform, some crowded round an object leaning against a suitcase which was being guarded by a policeman. It was Gold's blood-stained umbrella.

At Brighton Station the royal party – Prince Albert, his wife and their three daughters – were met by a hundred smart sailor lads in white jackets with rifles at their shoulder, headed by a band. After the mayor's welcoming speech, the lengthy procession wended its way through the packed streets towards the Hospital for Sick Children which the prince had come to officially open.

All the shops were shut and the royal route was decorated with crystal crowns, plumes, standards and gas illuminations. The greatest portion of the decorations were mottoes and monograms giving expression to loyal sentiments and expressions of welcome. Some were written in Danish, the nationality of the prince's wife, Alexandra. One was impertinent. It read, 'Next Time Bring Your Mother', a clear reference to Queen Victoria's known reluctance to visit the town.

All along the route masses of people lined the pavements and continually cheered the royal visitors, whose recognition became the signal for renewed cheers. Red was the prevailing colour in the thousands upon thousands of three-cornered flags that floated for a good five miles of Brighton thoroughfares.

When the royal party arrived at the hospital every window in view was occupied by people loyally waving handkerchiefs. While they were shown round the wards, a band played unceasingly outside and was not easily silenced. The mayor – who was resplendent in scarlet and gold and therefore repeatedly mistaken by the crowd for the prince (who wore a grey hat, light grey overcoat and carried an umbrella) – had to wave his hand several times before they finally stopped playing. After Prince Albert had declared the hospital open, a string of dignitaries presented 'purses' with donations for the hospital to his wife, Alexandra. Among them was Mrs Nye Chart. The prince appeared to take a special interest in her. The ceremony over, the royal party returned to the railway station and caught the train to London.

In the evening the whole of the sea front was crowded as people enjoyed the cooler air and looked at the boats and bathing machines which were decorated in bunting and at the lines of streamers that went from the seafront hotels down to the beach. Illuminations from a firework display on the West Pier, watched by thousands, glowed in the tender twilight amidst glimmering stars. At nine o'clock the Brighton Bonfire

Boys led a torchlight procession consisting of six to seven hundred people through the town, and the principal streets were a blaze of light until midnight, while the Brighton Pavilion remained open until the small hours of the morning to enable people to look at its decorations of gas lights, silver stars and Chinese lanterns of every shade and shape.

The following day some newspapers contrasted the silent welcome given to the lonely youth at Cuckfield with the rapturous one given to the Prince of Wales at Brighton. Hardly could there ever have been a greater contrast between the situation and status of two men.

Not surprisingly, Lefroy returned to Lewes in a depressed state and was placed in the infirmary because of a racking cough. He had not revealed any startling evidence which could prove the existence of a 'third man'. On leaving the courtroom he had even admitted to his solicitor, Dutton, that 'it looks very hot against me'.

But there was one piece of news that offered hope to Lefroy. On the day the enquiry ended, Dutton received a communication from the clerk to the Cuckfield magistrates. It enclosed a letter addressed 'To the Head Magistrate of Lewes'. It had the signature 'J. Major' attached and it mentioned the name of the alleged 'third man' in the railway carriage. The letter said he lived in Penzance, Cornwall. Dutton decided to write to the chief of police at Penzance to find out more about 'Mr J. Major' and he passed on the letter to Scotland Yard.

11

While awaiting his trial Lefroy continued to share his cell with two other prisoners. One of them, J. Foster, was released after a few weeks and gave a detailed account of their time together in prison to the *Daily Chronicle*:

When we sat down to the evening meal I remarked 'Lefroy is here somewhere isn't he? I wonder in what part of the prison he is placed.' Lefroy then laughed, and said 'They have put me in here for him', and I replied, 'Well, I should never have taken you for a man who could have done that sort of thing.' He pulled his sleeve up, and showed us his arm, asking, 'Does that look like killing a strong man?' His arm was as slender as a girl's. He always stuck to the idea that there was a third person in the carriage.

I told him that if I had been in his position, I should have made an endeavour to escape from the police at Brighton and rowed out to sea about a mile and a half, and got on board the first outward-bound ship that came by. Lefroy replied that he had thought of that, but that he could not get away from the detective who had to look after him and take him back to Mrs Clayton's. I asked him how he got to London from Wallington, when he left his cousin's house. He said that walk was the worst thing he had ever had to endure. During the journey he sat on one of the bridges for four hours, tired and worn out. When he reached London he went to a friend and got some money.

I was, as a rule, in bed long before Lefroy. Sometimes I have offered to make his bed for him, but he would never let me, saying that he would rather do it himself. He never did it properly, and, in fact, did not seem to know how to do anything in the shape of work. He would tell us that a nobleman married his cousin, and would also narrate to us incidents in connection with his life, and would delight us telling tales of his experiences in the Isle of Wight and Australia. He said he went out to the latter to do something with a dramatic company. I am sure he would have written the history of his life if I had asked him.

He seldom spoke of his father and mother, and only said they were dead, and he was glad of it because this would trouble them. He said the only people he had to think about were his two sisters.

He seemed to have very strong family affections, and one day after he had seen his sister, he came and sat in the armchair, at the foot of the bed, and for about five minutes he seemed unable to speak. Afterwards he said, 'it will kill my sister'. I never saw him cry, but that day he seemed almost broken-hearted. He used to have a good many visitors come to see him. His sister had been several times, and his solicitor's clerk several times.

He was very fond of the governor, of the doctor, and of Luton, the warder, who looked after us. We always used to know what the doctor would say. He always asked Lefroy 'Have you spit any blood?' The doctor had a very genial and pleasant manner. The Governor came round every morning at eleven, and would see we had all we wanted and that everything was right. He would ask Lefroy how he felt. At one time, a couple of weeks before his trial, he seemed in low spirits for a day or two, but this was owing to a cold which he caught sitting at an open window. He would insist on having that open, and I told him before that just before the time he wanted his strength most, he would be getting a cold. Under this cold he became depressed but never morose. He suffered from a lingering consumption, and had a slight cough. We used to have a little fun with Luton sometimes. One day we asked him for a latchkey as we would like to take a walk to Brighton. Luton said he did not think he could find any keys to fit the locks.

Lefroy used to have the newspapers sent to him. They were always a day old, and were sent from Mr Seale at Wallington. Anything relating to Lefroy was taken out by the Governor. We used to have a library book each every Monday, and after I had read mine I would change with him, and the same with Morris [another prisoner], so it was like having three books each week. He used to like reading history. The chaplain would always stop novels which were sent to him. I was there about a week when the novels were stopped. We knew there was one at the office, and at last we got it, but we had no more. He was rather angry and said there was no harm in it. The last book he had to read was *The History of Queen Boadicea*.

He neglected the Bible, and I thought that one in his position should not do so. I once told him to read the 37th Psalm, where we are taught to put our trust in God, and to believe in the excellency of His mercies. I thought the passage was fitted to his case, and the reading of it seemed to make an impression on him, for after he had finished he said he felt he must do something serious. I replied, 'then slap the book through the window,' and he did it. Whether he intended it to go through the window or not I cannot tell. It broke one or two panes of glass however. The next day he apologised to the Governor for what he had done. Lefroy, I believe, used to go to church simply because he was compelled, although he did say it passed the time. He would take a bible and prayer book but scarcely ever looked at them. It was simply a matter of form with him. We were each of us supposed to take the books.

When I was with him he had conceived a prejudice against the Chaplain because he believed he had prejudged the case. They were not very good friends. I believe he refused the advice of the minister and hardly treated him with courtesy. The day before I left, the Chaplain said to him, 'I shall have something to say to you when you come back [after your trial]'. Lefroy took that up as meaning that the Chaplain already condemned him, and afterwards said, 'I would rather chop off my hand quite off than speak to him again.' He couldn't bear him.

I remember on one occasion – although he held that he would surely disprove his guilt – assuming the probability of his being condemned, and I asked him what he thought about the matter. He said, 'If I am condemned, I will face death like a man; it will not put me out.' Lefroy always said that he was quite prepared to die, and his only regret seemed to be for his sisters, who, he said, would be disgraced by his death. He believed in Hell. I cannot reconcile that with the fact that he had no fear of death, but certainly he did not seem to be afraid of eternal punishment. I believe he had made up his mind not to dread death. He was a singularly determined character, and it is my opinion that when once he made up his mind to a thing, he would stick to it. This, I feel sure, was the reason of his being convinced that he would be able to clear himself of the charge, and it would also account for his being confident that he could make his escape from gaol. I told him if he could cut partly through several bars, and then break them off with the leg of a bedstead, he might be able to make his escape. One night he took the leg of my bedstead, but whether he did it in fun or with the intention of trying the bars I cannot say. He used to put all kinds of things in my bed at night, and likewise in Morris's. He was of a restless nature and was always up to something.

With respect to his veracity, he was not quite accurate in all the things he said. He used to contradict himself occasionally, and when I told him of it he was sometimes angry. I was, however, never with a nicer chap in my life. He was always up to some practical jokes, especially with my hat.

I can assure you we had some fine doings. Talk about a prison! If it was not for the confinement, you would hardly think it was one. I scarcely touched prison fare while I was there. Lefroy was kept well supplied with hampers, and all sorts of luxuries, except of course alcoholic liquors. And I can tell you, as a fact, that Lefroy is related by marriage to a certain noble earl, from whose cook came an elaborate supply of everything in the shape of eatables. I should say a seemingly more kind-hearted young fellow does not breathe. No one could possibly believe him guilty of murder. Whatever came into prison to him was as much ours as his. We were up to all sorts of tricks in the gaol. You certainly would never think that one of us was a man who stood in peril of his life with a horrible charge of murder hanging over his head, for although we were all as merry as crickets, he was the liveliest of the lot.

In speaking of cricket, cricket was of course our chief fun everyday. You see this tall hat of mine with the bulges in it? Of course we wore our ordinary clothes, and not the prison dress. We used to make this hat the wicket, get a bed lath [a long strip of wood] for the bat, and Lefroy taking off his stockings, we used to roll them into a ball, and have rare fun.

We used to have concerts, too, when we were tired of cricket. Lefroy did not sing, as he was no singer, so I supplied the vocalisations, and we used to make music with our hair combs, putting a piece of paper over the combs, and in this way blowing our jigs and songs in the most capital tunes in the most enjoyable way. He was very fond of music, and if he could hear any in the distance he would get to the window and open it. We were never interfered with. No, it is very different with people who are waiting their trial and those convicted. Lefroy was also a capital hand at making cigarettes – in fact I never knew better. We used to smoke cigarettes at night time. We had no tobacco but we had plenty of the best tea – more than we could use – which was sent in by his high station friends. He used to take the tea and roll it up in thin paper, and we had splendid cigarettes. During our concerts and our recitations we would smoke away in fine style, from eight until ten o'clock, and the warders never came to interrupt us. Although they saw the gaslight in our place, they never interfered with us.

I don't mind saying, too, that there was a great deal more in the food which used to be sent in than used always to appear to the eyes of the Governor and the wardens. I remember taking up a plumcake one day that had been sent in to Lefroy, and, on breaking it asunder, finding four half crowns in the centre. He seemed to sleep sound through the night and, in fact, I never knew him to wake up more than once. He was a most restless fellow unless when writing or reading. But his restlessness seemed to come from real good nature, and to be boiling over with a love of saying smart things, and practical joking. One day he got this hat I am wearing, and he and Morris poured a tin of condensed milk into it; you can see the marks now. That seemed to amuse him mightily.

He is undoubtedly a well-educated fellow, and knows how to use his tongue. I can assure you he used to say that in prison he was never more comfortable in his life, and as we were carrying on our games, and enjoying all the good things which were sent in to him, he used to say he would not mind having two years of that kind of thing – he was getting used to it.

He was very generous, and would give away anything he had. He offered me some of his new pocket handkerchiefs, but I told him he would want them at his trial. He then said that, if it would do me any good, I might make what use I liked of what I had heard there [in prison]. Acting upon that, I feel, in thus conveying this to the public, I am not doing anything Lefroy would wish to be undone, and making known anything he would be afraid of becoming public. He did not care about life at all. That was owing, in my opinion, to his disease. He never looked forward to a long life. I told him once that I did not think, if he did get off, that he would live long. He answered that he did not suppose that he would. He seemed to think that it was only anticipating by a short time that which must have come. He did not seem to have regretted the life he had spent. I said to him that if I had my life over again I would go on differently. He said, 'You must not look back. Looking back on impossibilities is a disease of the mind.' He used to act upon that principle.

He also said that life was not worth living for, and that but for the disgrace, it mattered very little how one died, because when life was gone it was gone, and there was an end of it. He said that several times. . . Here is a letter which I have received from him since I have been out. He told me to 'beware of the vidders'. The meaning of that is that I jokingly told him there were 27 widows in Hastings, each one of whom were anxiously waiting my coming out with the desire to marry me. He was very fond of me, and was like a brother. I told him the history of my life, and he was very interested. I used to look after the food and that, I was like a valet to him. When they separated us I shook hands and parted from him. I don't think he was insane; he was too clever to be insane. He himself laughed at the idea. He hardly ever mentioned Mr Gold, and when he did it was when I brought it up.

The extract again shows Lefroy partially living in a fantasy world. Foster's assertion that Lefroy did not like the chaplain may be incorrect, however, for on August 8th Lefroy had written to his sister, Mary Brickwood: 'I saw the Chaplain yesterday for the first time, and I liked him very much. When General Lefroy [his uncle] was living at Blackheath the chaplain knew him very well. In spite of the terrible charge against me, I am happy here, and were God's hand to strike me down now, I should fear no fear; my mind is at rest - rest that comes from innocence, and from that alone.'

Some of his most affectionate letters were to his 40-year-old cousin Anne Clayton, to whom he continued to maintain his innocence. On August 16th , he wrote:

My dearest Annie,
The time that I think of you most, dear, is during our long nights in bed, from 8.30pm until 6 am. Then my mind, in the stillness of the night, wanders back, carries me out once more to life and freedom, and to you. Bitter thoughts against God rise up in my mind, and I try in vain to divine why I have been thus cruelly afflicted by Him. Possibly, from my past life I may have deserved this awful punishment, but after all my sins have been more of omission than commission. My years but a boy's – so does not this fearful chastisement seem out of proportion to my offence? Annie, Dearest, shall I ever see the silver lining of the clouds again? In any case, however, I must be – say, I am – far happier than the wretched man, who has escaped the hands of justice, and left an ill-fated fellow creature to suffer in his stead. At least, however, One Judge has already acquitted me of the awful crime with which I have been charged.

On September 6th:

You say, dear, that public opinion, that thing of treachery, is beginning to imagine there may be two sides, to any question, even mine. All I care is that if such be the case, as showing that the principle of fair-play is not yet a stranger to English minds as I had imagined it to be. Often, when the stillness of the night is around me, I think of you all and shed many a bitter tear of sorrow and strange anomaly! Of joy; sorrow at the thought of what I might have been to you all, and tears of gladness that at least my Creator and myself know that I am not that which most men believe and say. Around us all is gloom, dearest but 'be not afraid, for joy cometh in the morning'.

On September 24th:

Do not judge my feelings towards you and all I love by the tone of my letters, for my heart is too full sometimes even to put pen to paper. I never cease this thinking of you, whom I can trust in all. Very often my want of feeling has been commented upon by the Press and ministers of religion. I have been termed callous, defiant, and reckless, caring neither for those laws of God and man, which they accuse me of breaking, whereas, if only they once drew aside the veil of prejudice, they would perhaps admit that my sustaining power might after all be a sense of innocence. Your dear letter, indeed, gave me great pleasure. Rest assured that I have never for a moment doubted your belief in my innocence. It has been the one thought that has sustained me during the terrible time of imprisonment. My heart nearly breaks when I think of the sacrifices you are making for one who, however much he loved and loves, has done so little for you; but God will, I trust and believe repay you all.

You cannot imagine how often I think of you all. Two faces in particular – yours and another's – are ever before my eyes, telling me, hope on and hope ever . . .

Whose was the other face?

12

Lefroy's trial was set to take place at Maidstone in November, so there was time for his lawyer to find evidence to save him from the hangman's rope. But things were not looking good. In August, Lefroy's solicitor, Dutton, spent three days in the west country investigating the letter purporting to come from the 'third person', J.Major. He discovered that Inspector Swanson was also there for the same purpose. Eventually, Dutton received a letter from the chief constable of Penzance, dated 13th August:

> Sir,
> In reply to yours of the 10th inst., purporting to be written by Mr J Major, Chapel Street, Penzance. I find there is a Mr M. Major and a Mr J. B. Major, father and son, residing at that address. I have seen them both this morning, and they state that they know nothing of the said letter, nor of the person named therein . . . Mr M. Major returned here last night from London. He left for London on 26th July, 1881, which appears to be the date of the said letter.

Afterwards, Dutton was still publicly optimistic about finding the 'third person' before the trial. He told reporters he felt he could disprove the evidence of the pawnbrokers and the assertion that Gold never carried firearms while travelling. Moreover, Lefroy's friends claimed that there were good reasons for his flight from Wallington on the night of the crime. They argued that as there were a couple of outstanding warrants against him – probably relating to his past frauds – he feared they would be brought out against him if he remained in Wallington.

This apprehension, coupled with his fraud regarding the passing of the Hanoverian coins on the morning of the murder, offered a sufficient explanation for his behaviour. But the best news of all for Lefroy was that his family – at great financial sacrifice – had managed to procure the services of one of the most successful defence barristers of the era, Montagu Williams.

Within months of returning from Australia, Lefroy started to contribute short articles to his local paper, the *Sutton and Wallington Herald*, but his attempts to get into the theatre were less successful. While Lefroy was hiding in Stepney, Frederick Maccabe – the 'King of Mimics' and a famous ventriloquist who often played two characters at once (male and female, in which he was dressed half on one side as a man and half on the other as a woman and spoke alternately in a male and female voice) – had given an interview to the *Daily Chronicle* just before leaving on the Lusitania for a tour of Australia:

> I have known the man for a long time, but always under the name of Mapleton. He introduced himself to me by showing me a copy of the *Era* containing a criticism which he said he had written. His object seemed always to show that he was connected with journalism and the theatrical profession. In the Gaiety Restaurant, in the street and other places he has seized me by the button of my coat, and I have often felt inclined to cut the button off and leave it in his possession. I never knew anyone who had such a tenacity of purpose in getting hold of and sticking to your button. I have been subject to the unpleasant operation many times, and on every possible occasion I have avoided him. His main purpose appeared to be to raise money on the strength of a promise to 'write something favourable,' a circumstance which to me was sufficient evidence that he had no connection beyond that of an amateur with journalism.
>
> During my season last year [1880] at St James's Hall, London, I arrived at a just estimate of his true character, when he added as an inducement for me to engage him to write something for me to produce, 'I can work the Press for you'. Experience then told me that this man did not belong to the journalistic profession and never have I seen him in the company of any recognized Pressmen. Upon the second time he button-holed me he requested the loan of £5, saying he should write something for me, and that I might deduct the amount from the price to be paid. I declined to comply with the request.
>
> He continued to pester me, but without any pecuniary reward, and at St James's Hall last autumn he thrust himself up the private staircase to the door of my dressing room. He said he particularly wished to see me, upon which I referred him to my manager. He persisted, however, in endeavouring to get an interview with me, but knowing the inflictions I had previously received, I managed, though with difficulty, to escape from him by locking the door and hurrying on to the stage. The man thoroughly haunted me, and when he found it impossible to get an interview he sent me a manuscript of a farce, with a letter describing the composition as being one of the best farces ever written, and exactly suitable to my

'style'. I read the manuscript out of curiosity and found the farce utterly worthless, far worse than might be expected from the author. Mapleton or Lefroy was one of the most extraordinary men I have ever met. What struck me most was that he would never look me straight in the face, his eyes never remained on any part of one's face for more than an instant. He talked with his eyes looking down, apparently afraid of his eyes meeting those of anyone else. He professes to know all actors and journalists but is unknown by them. He was a mystery. A man who kept chattering like a magpie to you and ignored what you said to him.

About a year before the murder Lefroy visited the office of an important weekly paper and requested to see the editor. He was told to leave his visiting card. He left it with the following note:

Dear Sir,
I regret exceedingly that you decline to see me, as I wished to bring under your notice a subject of remarkable interest, that I propose to deal with in a masterly article, and I should be glad to place it at your disposal. However, on a future occasion we may be able to go into the matter. In the meantime, I beg to leave to your consideration two or three short sketches, which I hope you may be able to use, and I will take the liberty of calling upon you next Monday week.

The editor looked at the sketches but decided they were not good enough and told him so on the Monday.

In November 1880, however, Lefroy got a break. Adopting the nom de plume Arthur Lefroy (he dared not use his own name, which was already familiar to the readers of the *Era*), he was commissioned by Alfred Stanton, the owner of the Croydon Theatre, to write the Christmas pantomime. It was reported that he attended most of the rehearsals, although he barely made a single suggestion.

Robinson Crusoe by Arthur Lefroy received good reviews despite, according to one local paper, its similarity to a version written by one of his acquaintances, Robert Reece, a well-known librettist.

Mr A. Lefroy has furnished the actors with some excellent lines to speak, and some most humourous ditties to sing as they go. . . In short, Mr Lefroy has made a right pleasant story of the mingling of many of the ancient friends of our juvenile days, and it never fails to interest. Considering the youth and experience of the author, he shows marked ability. Taken altogether the production is a credit to all concerned in it and we hope to see it gain the large measure of support its many sterling merits ought to receive.

(*Croydon Times* 1/1/1881)

Stanton told the *Era* that: 'during the first week the pantomime has drawn wonderfully good houses; in fact, it is some years since we did anything like such good business as we are doing now.' Unfortunately the snow storms of January, which proved so fatal to theatrical enterprises all over the country, curtailed its run. But, as Lefroy himself said, at last his 'foot was on the first rung of the ladder'. He now started to write at every available opportunity but all his manuscripts were returned and not used.

Earlier that year, in the wake of Disraeli's death, Lefroy had sent an article 'The Future of the Conservative Party' to several liberal newspapers. In it, he had made his politics clear:

In short, Conservatism pure and simple is to get into office as soon, and to stay there as long as possible. Of course, when in office the Tories do a certain amount of work for the sake of appearances, but they take good care that while it tickles the vanity of many, it shall benefit none – never minding what care, poverty, and want there may be at home, as long as they can extort taxes from the people to spend in unrighteous and unnecessary wars abroad.

But the people of Britain are beginning now to wake from their lethargic sleep, and discover themselves what manner of creature this conservatism really is. The mighty stream of progress is daily – nay, hourly – gaining ground, and ere long all the fetters of bigotry, superstition, and ignorance, forged in the gloomy bygone days of long ago upon a sleeping people, will be swept away by its mighty torrent, and conservatism with all its cant and falsehood, will be carried ruthlessly away – down, down to the dark unfathomable depths of well deserved oblivion.

Lefroy was undoubtedly influenced politically and as a writer by his favourite author: George R. Sims. Sims was a very successful playwright, newspaper columnist, public speaker and radical social reformer who, two years later, would unmask a less pleasant side of Victorian society in his book, *How the Poor Live*.

As he became more desperate for success Lefroy decided to write to newspaper editors claiming that he was the relation of some person who was well known to them, but who, of course, was dead. One example was a letter he wrote on April 24th 1881:

Dear Sir,

Might I ask you as a great favour whether or not you could find me employment on the 'Newcastle Chronicle'. I have considerable experience on several of the United States Radical journals. I am a brilliant leader writer and a good hand at satirical poems, and in addition I am thoroughly acquainted with all the dramatic doings of the day, being a member of some of the leading literary and dramatic clubs. I should be glad to arrange on very moderate terms, and ask only for a trial for the sake of the good services of my uncle, the late Richard Cobden, rendered to Liberalism.

I am, dear sir, yours faithfully, Arthur Lefroy.

This scheme failed and so he decided to go on an entirely new tack altogether. He wrote letters to several well-known theatrical figures, coached in the same strain as before but now saying that he was related to the late eminent actor Mr Charles Harcourt. But over this he almost got his fingers burned, for Mrs Harcourt and her husband's bosom friend, Thomas Mowbray, invited him for tea. They plied him with all sorts of questions to which he had to give lying answers and he only backed out of a tricky situation by promising to lay before them proof of his identity when the July mail arrived from Sydney. He quickly abandoned this scheme.

Locally, Lefroy was a well known figure. Five days after the murder, the *Croydon Advertiser and Surrey County Reporter* (2/7/1881) included the following report:

Lefroy or Mapleton was well known in Croydon and the district of Carshalton and Wallington. His height is about five feet eight inches and his stooping shoulders made him appear shorter. His walk will not be easily forgotten, as the action of the left leg is rather awkward, the limb being slightly thrown out as he walked, which rendered his gait a trifle shambling. His face is habitually pale, giving the idea that his constitution is not one of the strongest, and his features easy of remembrance.

He seldom laughed. When he smiled he rather affected a smile which exposed his spoilt teeth and rather prominent gums. His cheeks are hollowed, and sink away towards a chin which boasts no prominence whatever, and furtive dreamy grey eyes overshadowed with eyebrows nearly meeting on the forehead and inclining to shagginess, give him a careworn expression seldom found in a young man. Without dressing shabbily, he was never swellishly attired.

When going to Croydon or town he frequently wore a black frock or cut-away coat, and on many evenings he has been met leaving Wallington station in evening dress, wearing above it a light overcoat. At no time could he be said to have dressed himself with care as would a man who took pride in clothes.

He was a most agreeable companion. And his information on theatricals and his interest therein was always large: although it may be said that in imparting information he sometimes took strange flights of fancy. On first introduction he saluted his new acquaintance with an air of uneasy deference that imparted the idea that he was of youthful years and of unusually modest and retiring nature. But in renewed intercourse he seemed to gain confidence, and then, while the notion that he was still young remained, it was not difficult to find that his knowledge of the world was extensive.

He comported himself as a well-bred young fellow. His language too, was always temperate, and he was besides very abstemious in the matter of drink, generally, when drinking with an acquaintance, taking the smallest quantity of brandy and water procurable, and resolutely refusing to partake of more . . . it may be stated that he sought the present writer in Croydon (which place he had left for the day) on Boxing Day last, and on meeting him on the following day deplored the fact that he could not find him, inasmuch as he desired him to write the Boxing Night notice of the Covent Garden pantomime for the sporting and dramatic paper referred to, his own hands being too full to accomplish all the work imposed upon him.

Lefroy's chief thought was to approach leading literary figures and win their esteem by getting a play or an article accepted. He wrote to famous people such as George Grossmith and Henry Bracy, the comic tenor, and got to know several theatrical personalities. He seems to have been well liked, and when in funds was considered to be extremely generous. On his 21st birthday, in February 1881, he inherited £35 from his mother's estate and, although short of money himself, gave some of it to his older sister Mary who was bringing up six children on her own.

In early spring he lost his job writing about 'local celebrities' for the *Herald* and started to tell friends he was working for the *Era*, borrowing money on the strength of it. On March 22nd he wrote to the journal:

It may interest some of your numerous readers to know that in addition to the list of M. Offenbach's published and unpublished works already given in your column, another production of the great opera composer is in existence, a fact not at present known to half a dozen persons. This opera-comique is in three acts, and is entitled *La Reine Lucette*, or perhaps more properly Lucette. It was written twelve years ago, and immediately on completion was privately published by Mr Frank Coppin, of Melbourne. The plot of the piece turns upon the adventures of a young French girl on an enchanted island, and the music has been pronounced by the few who have heard it in M. Offenbach's best vein; that is to say music more of La Grande Duchess type than that of the Tambour Major M. Offenbach, prior to his death, made strenuous efforts to repurchase it from Mr Coppin, but without success, that gentleman having resolved to produce it, if possible, first of all in Australia. But, owing to the force of circumstance, he has abandoned the idea, and I have every reason to believe that during the coming Autumn the London Public and the Profession will have an opportunity of passing judgement upon one of the great Franch composer's works.

Apologising on your valuable space. I am, sirs. Yours faithfully, Arthur Lefroy.

Lefroy told friends that Frank Coppin was a fabulously rich sheep farmer who had chosen him as his protege. A few weeks later Lefroy wrote to Henry Bracy, claiming that Coppin was dead and had left him the opera plus £1,000 a year. If he married, this figure would increase to £10,000. He offered to give Bracy the opera at the end of May in gratitude for his friendship, saying he was going to give up journalism and go into Parliament. But there was no Frank Coppin (although there *was* a famous actor manager, *George* Coppin at the Theatre Royal in Melbourne) and there was no opera called *La Reine Lucette*.

Sims recalled in his autobiography, *My Life: Sixty Years Recollections of Bohemian London*, that Lefroy had actually come to see him a few weeks before the murder with the name of Mapleton on his card, but he had been out of town at the time. Instead, Lefroy saw his friend George Spencer Edwards, the editor of the *Era*, and told him that he had bought a revolver in order to commit suicide if he failed to sell his play.

However, the false life Lefroy was leading was expensive and taking its toll. In the weeks leading up to the murder he became more and more depressed and desperate. On May 20th, he wrote to a friend in Wallington seeking yet another loan on the strength of his 'job' with the *Era*:

During my residence in Wallington, I have led, as you know, not a particularly happy life. Of relatives, I have really none, and I am as nearly destitute of friends, having none, in fact, but yourself.

Through the force of circumstances, I have been unable to pay you yet the 35s I owe you. You, fortunately, perhaps have never felt what it is like to be pressed for a few shillings – have never had to fight your way through the rank and file of journalism unfriended and alone, no one to give you a helping hand; while, if you fall, your place is instantly filled up as if you never existed. It is only those who have passed, to a certain extent, through this cruel ordeal that can feel as I feel now.

My greatest fear is, however, that your natural refusal to help me with a loan will also be followed by the loss of your friendship.

In early June 1881, he organised a cricket match at which it was alleged he stole money from several of the participants' bags while they were on the field of play. A week before the murder he had an interview with a publishing company but was turned down because of his shabby appearance. He had now sold nearly all his clothes and was in debt to his family and friends. So, leading up to the trial, the image of Lefroy was that of a man who was a liar, a fraudster and probably a murderer, too. The police believed so. Their only doubt was, had he acted alone?

On Friday, October 28th Lefroy was taken by coach to Barcombe Station. He looked pale but was smartly dressed in dark trousers, black coat, a high hat and new shoes. As the train was late, he sat in the waiting room with two warders in front of an open fire. News of his presence quickly spread and people came in pretending to look for the station master, but really to look at him. Once on the train – in a reserved carriage – Lefroy overheard other travellers making derogatory comments about him and, turning to one of the warders, said, 'Well, if all are of the same opinion as these people, I will not have much chance of being acquitted.'

At Maidstone, he was confined in the county prison, which was attached to a long unpretentious stone building – the courthouse. As at Lewes, his family was allowed to bring him in food to eat and he was provided with library books. But he was very much alone, and even in the chapel and the exercise yard he was screened from the other prisoners.

In the days before the trial, the whole town was buzzing with intense excitement. The local newspapers even promised to publish extra editions to cover the town's 'event of the century'. Special excursion trains from London were organised for those who wanted to attend the trial. The *Times* (2/11/1881) commented:

Crimes of violence are so frequent that a murder four months ago usually slips out of the memory. It is not so with respect to the charge against Lefroy. The murder was so terrible, the circumstances were so peculiar, the escape and capture of Lefroy was so much out of routine that the facts are still fresh in the recollections of everyone in every household in the land.

The gathering of court officials and witnesses alone amounted to more than a hundred people. The jury – all of whose surnames began with H – were booked into a hotel opposite the courthouse and were provided with 'meat, drink, and candle and such other necessaries as the law allowed'. Strictly guarded, they were not allowed to talk to anyone.

At the railway station, small knots of people could be seen looking at a new object of curiosity: a railway carriage with a tarpaulin thrown across its centre. The cover hid from public view a by now famous train compartment. Still visible though were the dry blood stains upon the footboard at the side at which it was conjectured that the body of the murdered man was thrown out of the carriage.

The day before the trial started there was a murky, heavy and dull atmosphere in Maidstone. Outside the court building, a persistent downpour of rain made business bad for the traders owning the oyster barrows; the sausage and baked potato men and the nut sellers. Towards the evening they beat a hasty retreat in the face of the pelting rain and want of customers. They were consoled by the thought that they would do good business in the morning.

Dutton visited the prisoner in his cell. When he left he told the 50 or so waiting reporters – some representing foreign newspapers – that Lefroy was optimistic and was pleased with his defence team. In the evening Lefroy wrote to his sister Mary:

> My dearest M,
>
> I have no fear whatever of the trial, whatever the result may be. I feel as if I were going into a great battle, from which, by God's grace, I may return unharmed. I have every confidence in my counsel. The evidence I shall be able to produce will do much, and believe me, dearest, or not, there is a possibility of the real murderer being arrested or at least identified before the week is out. Mention this to no one not even Dutton, for reasons he will explain when he sees you.
>
> Love Percy.

13

Maidstone Courthouse, Friday 4th November 1881.

A cold driving, drenching rain, that obscured the air as effectively as a 'Scotch mist',and cast gloom over the town, ushered in the first day of the trial. At a quarter past eight, a detachment of police marched up to the court building and began to make preparations. At the station, the 'special' excursion trains from London began unloading their passengers. They joined the hundreds of country folk who had trekked in from the surrounding villages. By 9 o'clock, an hour before the trial was due to start, a large army of people, ankle deep in mud and soaked to the skin, stood outside the courthouse waiting patiently to hear or see something of Lefroy.

Shortly, the judge, Lord Coleridge, Chief Justice of England, passed into the building amid the blare of trumpets, blown by blue-coated cock-hatted functionaries. He was followed by witnesses, officials and reporters and, finally, by the public scrambling for seats. The vast majority of the crowd, however, remained outside for most of the day, watching the bold facade of the building with curious interest.

At 10 o'clock Coleridge, resplendent in ermine and scarlet and looking like an aristocratic coachman, entered and took his seat on the bench. A few seconds later a man standing at the top of the stairs in the dock gave a signal and the prisoner, who had been waiting in the underground passage below, was brought up the stairs. In the midst of a strained and expectant silence, Lefroy slowly and dramatically entered the courtroom accompanied by a chaplain and two warders:

> With every eye fixed upon him, but without faltering in the slightest, he emerged into view, advanced to the front of the stage and bowed. His stage – an irregular four-sided space, hemmed in on every side by iron spikes, rigidly guarded by policemen, and furnished with but three of four wooden chairs – a kind of cage similar to that in which wild beasts are confined. Stay, there was on one chair something to indicate consideration – it was the only thing and deserves notice. A green foot hassock had been placed upon the rough seat and it was for the latest arrival in the court that the hassock had been placed.
>
> (*Daily Telegraph* 5/11/1881)

He was wearing a tightly buttoned up frock-coat with a dark cravat round his neck. In his hand, he carried a brand new silk hat, bought by a friend. Before him he surveyed an imposing display of the paraphernalia of justice – an immense array of officials, jury, judge, solicitors, together with reporters and spectators, all straining to catch a glimpse of him. What a contrast it was from the stillness of the prison cell and corridors which he had just left behind.

Lord Coleridge surveyed Lefroy intently through an eyeglass for some moments and read out the court calendar which described him as a 'journalist' and his education as 'reads and writes well'. When asked to plead to the indictment, 'for the wilful murder of Frederick Isaac Gold upon June 27', Lefroy replied, in a voice so inaudible that it was almost a whisper, 'I plead what I am, and that is not guilty'.

The attorney general, Sir Henry James, with a pile of documents beside him, outlined the case for the prosecution. There was, he said, a 'chain' of evidence which pointed to Lefroy's guilt and implied that the murder was premeditated. He concluded his speech by declaring:

> Without doubt the prisoner was in the carriage in which the deadly deed was done, and he had the means of committing the murder, and was found with the dead man's watch in his shoe. It was suggested that there was a third person in the carriage, who had first struck him down insensibly and then committed the murder. But, if so, how was it that he put the murdered man's watch in his shoe? And still more, what had become of that watch? How came the prisoner to have it, and why was it he did not produce it now? And why was it he did not prefer an accusation against the murderer, but took to flight and concealed himself? The jury must judge whether there could be any reason for this except the consciousness of guilt.
>
> I only ask you the jury to deal with the case by the light of common sense, and if the facts lead you clearly to the conclusion that the prisoner committed the murder, then you must not shrink from your duty in saying so by your verdict.

There were over 70 witnesses for the prosecution in all, including policemen, railway officials, watchmakers, pawnbrokers, doctors, labourers, train passengers and even members of Lefroy's own family.

One of the first to testify was a woman in her sixties, dressed in black with a long crepe veil over her bonnet. On her appearance a suppressed murmur and a craning of necks on the part of those at the back of the court took place. It was Mrs Lydia Gold. When she entered the box Lefroy gave her a sharp, penetrating eager glance. She looked round. Their eyes met, and the prisoner's eyes dropped. He seemed visibly affected.

In a hushed, respectful silence, Mrs Gold recited the tale that was now so familiar to all. She identified one thing after another of her husband's possessions found on him or near the railway line: a broken chain, a piece of an eye-glass, an umbrella, a hat and a purse which he had when he left home. But she said she was surprised that his skull cap and a wallet which contained his railway ticket, one or two blank cheques and more valuable papers had not been found. She ended her testimony by telling the court she had never set eyes on the prisoner before. She confirmed, though, that her brother-in-law lived in Wallington.

The next witness, William Franks, a ticket collector at London Bridge Station, said he had seen Lefroy pace up and down the platform before entering Gold's compartment. Lefroy had difficulty opening the door and so Franks had done it for him. He described him as a 'thin man, rather sunburnt and sickly looking with a black moustache and a little tuft of whiskers at the side of his face'. He never saw a third person get into the carriage and denied that his description had been influenced by the photofit of Lefroy printed in the *Daily Telegraph*, which he claimed not to have seen.

Franks was fiercely cross-examined by Lefroy's lawyer, Montague Williams, who suggested Lefroy could have been looking for a lady friend (whom he had agreed to meet) and that Franks might not have been looking when a third person entered the compartment. Furthermore, Franks had said that Lefroy had been wearing a low hat and yet the booking clerk from the same station had said it was a high hat. Williams made the most of this material disagreement and at the end looked triumphantly at the jury. The attorney general intervened:

'To give such a look to the jury is most improper.'

'I did not give the look to the jury, but to you yourself!' replied Williams.

Thomas Watson, the guard on the train, testified that it had slowed to four miles an hour for a few seconds at Hassocks Gate – ten miles south of Balcombe tunnel – but that he had seen no one get out. This contradicted the evidence of the driver and the rear guard that the train had not slowed the whole journey. Watson was cross-examined by Williams.

'When did you first see Mr Gold?'

'I saw him in a First Class compartment at Croydon with a white pocket handkerchief thrown lightly over his head. I thought he was asleep.'

'Did you see anyone with him?'

'No.'

'What did you think of the prisoner when you first saw him at Preston Park Station?'

'When he told me that the people who had attacked him must have left the carriage on the way down, I did not believe him, but considered him to be a lunatic who had tried to commit suicide. Every part of his visible flesh was covered in blood.'

Watson admitted it was possible for a person to get out of a train at speed but thought that, at the very least, the person would suffer broken limbs. The judge asked him whether a man who left a train at 60 miles an hour would be able to run away and hide himself. To laughter in the public gallery, Watson replied that he thought he would stop where he got out.

The most controversial witness of the first day was a middle-aged Brighton councillor, Oliver Weston. He claimed to have seen Lefroy in the stationmaster's office at Brighton when he first arrived:

> I touched one of his eyebrows and said 'I say, my friend, this is not a gun wound. You were never shot at. These are mere prods with an umbrella'. And when I saw bloody finger prints on one side of his neck and a thumb mark on the other and pointed them out I said 'It must have been a hot struggle while it lasted'. I asked the railway officials what they were going to do with him. An official told me that he thought he was a lunatic. I said I didn't think he was and that he should be taken to the police station in a closed carriage. I thought he had committed some crime. I made this statement to my solicitor six weeks ago and was surprised that I was not called at the inquest or the magistrates' enquiry.

Williams sharply cross-examined Weston, telling him that no other railway officials remembered seeing him at the station, and he recalled three of them to confirm this fact. Williams also managed to undermine the evidence of a Mrs Ann Brown, who lived in a cottage near the railway line at Horley. She claimed that she and her daughter had seen two men fighting or 'larking about' as the train passed. Under cross-examination, she admitted that she had seen the train compartment only through a shut window in her house and did not remember how many people were in it.

Benjamin Hall, the Brighton doctor who had treated Lefroy, gave his evidence with an impressive air of accuracy, minutely describing the wounds on his face and head, which, as he observed, were all at the front and never at the back of his head:

Lefroy had six semi-circular wounds on the hair scalp; a small contused wound on the head and a graze on the back of the ear. There were no gunshot wounds. The barrel of a pistol, umbrella, or trigger of a pistol could have caused these wounds. His hair was matted with blood; his hands and neck smeared as if the blood had ran down from his head and been wiped. The blood on his face would have come from his wounds. That on his clothes from elsewhere. There was blood about the thighs and legs and the overcoat was almost saturated. I believe the wounds on the head of the prisoner could not have been self-inflicted.

A forensic surgeon, Mr Bond, believed that the terrible cuts on Gold's face might have been inflicted during Gold's attempts to stop his attacker from cutting his throat as he was fighting for his life on the floor of the compartment. Bond thought the bullet he had found in Gold's throat would have stunned him and weakened his powers of resistance. The other deep wounds on various parts of his body would have caused a lot of blood and could have been inflicted by a knife or a razor. During Bond's evidence, one person at the back of the court fainted and had to be carried out by one of the constables.

A reporter described the closing scenes of the first day:

The judge was busy, as the energy of his clerk as a sharpener of his Lordship's pencils testified. Counsel were busy; solicitors were alive to every turn of the case. The jury listened with unremitting attention. Reporters laboured hard to hear, and make notes. Artists worked away at the sketches they had produced of the court. Everybody was engaged save the individual who was more concerned than all beside in the eventual upshot of the proceedings, and he sat almost motionless, and with the air of one who was bored. The events of the day seemed to lack for him that interest which they apparently possessed for everybody else in the crowded court.

Night coming on, the court was lit, and owing to a curious arrangement of the lamps, the whole scene resembled a Rembrandtish picture. The rays fell upon the prisoner as he sat forward, his eyes partially closed, his arms folded. They fell, too, upon the upturned faces of the warders and others who were with him in the dock, and, occupying a line in rear of the chair he filled; they lighted upon the bright robes of the judge and the scarlet and gold uniform of the sheriff, on the white wigs of the counsel, and the glistening papers on the table; on the heads of the crowd, too, who filled the public gallery throwing the surroundings into a deep shade, and bathing whatever was prominent with a rich colouring of yellow. The gas must have been poor to have this particular effect but the effect was there, and it was strangely impressive.

(*Daily Telegraph* 5/11/1881)

A minute after the proceedings ended, Lefroy wheeled round and, ducking his head so as to avoid the gaze of the spectators, disappeared down the steps leading to his cell.

THE SECOND DAY

An hour before the trial was due to start, the public galleries were already full as Lefroy's innocence or guilt was eagerly discussed. One elderly gentleman, evidently of local importance, asserted that Lefroy was safe enough, an opinion with which those around did not entirely concur.

'Why?' asked a bystander.

'Because you can't hang on circumstantial evidence!' replied the dignitary.

The court began by listening to the witnesses who had seen Lefroy at Preston Park and Brighton. They were followed by Detective Sergeant Holmes, who gave the appearance of a man who expected the worst. He had to endure what he described later as the unhappiest half hour of his life as he struggled to account for his actions under harsh cross-examination by all the barristers. At one point, he tried to look dignified by holding onto the lapels of his coat but it merely looked as if he was trying to stop himself from falling down. Even Lefroy smiled as he watched the fruitless efforts of the baffled detective to appear at ease.

Although from his powerful build he might be of service in a street row, the power to track a crime or to put together a chain of facts which led to an inevitable conclusion was conspicuously wanting. This was painfully illustrated by such answers as 'I hasked him if he were in the 'abit of carrying firearms . . .. I hentered all he said in my report.' When the witness read his report it was evident that the grade he could have passed at Board School would hardly have been a high one.

(*Brighton Evening Argus* 6/11/1881)

After cross-examining Holmes, Williams sat down with an air of triumph after fully exposing the detective's failure to take his client into custody.

The court's merriment was by no means confined to the poor detective. When Mrs Nye Chart stepped into the witness box – dressed as if she had just come from the picnic she had enjoyed on 27th June – she barely kissed the Bible when taking the oath, and one of the court officials complained to the judge. What his lordship said was unclear, but the next witness gave the book a kiss that would have sufficed a dozen people.

Mr Ellis, who owned a stationer's shop in Wallington, hardly enhanced Holmes's reputation. This is what he told the court:

Shortly before eight o'clock on Monday morning (27th June), Mr Clayton's servant brought a note to my shop. It was in Lefroy's handwriting and was as follows: 'Would Mr Ellis come up as early as possible before 10.30, respecting a stationery order which Mrs Clayton wishes to give him'. As it was only three minutes away, I went to her house and was shown into the drawing room by the servant. Whilst waiting there, I heard Lefroy speaking in the lower part of the house and I also heard him passing up and down the stairs. Just as the servant entered the room and asked me to wait another five minutes, which I agreed to do, I heard the front gate click and looking out of the window, caught sight of Lefroy who was hurriedly leaving the house.

Another five minutes had elapsed when the servant brought me a list of articles required by Mrs Clayton which was also in Lefroy's handwriting. I then proceeded to my shop and was surprised on hearing from my lad that Lefroy had left some cash in an envelope in payment of his account – he owed about £1 7s – and that he (my lad) had given him 13s change. Upon opening the envelope I found it contained two Hanoverian coins. I immediately ran back to the house but was told Lefroy had gone. I didn't go to the police because I had known him a long time and thought that he must have placed the 'coins' in error. When I later contacted Mrs Clayton about 'her' order she said she knew nothing about it.

That night, I shut my shop at about a quarter to ten and went to see a friend, Mr Kedge, who was the stationmaster at Wallington. He told me that a detective had got Lefroy for suspected murder at 4 Cathcart Road. I went there and found Holmes waiting outside the house. I told him about Lefroy's fraud and asked him if he was in the house. Holmes said he was. I said, 'I thought you had him in custody?' to which Holmes replied, 'No, there is not sufficient grounds to charge him'. I told him to charge him on my account but he refused. I told the detective that there was no use waiting in the front as there was a back way and he went quickly there.

Ellis added that Lefroy had always been a good and well-mannered customer whose honesty he had never doubted.

During the morning, a young woman, sitting in the public gallery kept steadily at her needlework. Next to her another lady was busy at crochet work. Both paused in their activities whenever a new witness appeared. One man was engaged in making a sketch of Lefroy on his shirt cuff, and others were immersed in their newspapers. Not until a policeman produced the coat of the murdered man did everyone stop and take notice.

The bloodstains were deep and numerous, and the torn state of the garment seemed to be the best evidence of the last desperate struggle for life made by its late owner. Williams was exultant, for Lefroy's coat had not been torn at all and surely the struggle was so ferocious that the assailant's coat would have been torn also. However, the policeman dampened his enthusiasm by testifying that when they found Gold his coat had not been torn; but that in order to remove it, they had been forced to cut it away from the body, and this accounted for its tattered state.

The production of other relics of the case caused immense interest in the court – to everyone, that is, except Lefroy, who maintained his fixed position with a dreamy, half-wakeful look at the spiked rails in front of him. Only the blood-stained collar said to be his excited anything like marked attention from him. He seemed bored by the whole proceedings of which he was compelled to be a spectator. He was never alone in the dock:

Somehow or other, several persons – neither prisoners nor, by appearance, gaol officials – came into the dock by the staircase from below, and, being provided with seats, remained spectators of the scene. The governor of the gaol and the prison chaplain in a pew in one corner of the dock had a boy – comparatively speaking, a child – with them. The prisoner was flanked on each side, within an arm's length, by two people, the one couple facing the other, and sitting sideways to the bench.

One of the party, by his dress, was a clergyman, and another was a gentlemanly looking young man fashionably dressed, and playfully holding the railings of the dock with a gloved hand. Not even when the clergyman leaning rather heavily upon the back of the chair by his side, brought about a collapse of that portion of the chair, and, smiling at the disaster, handed the broken-off back to a gaoler, did Lefroy look up, or appear conscious of those by whom he was so closely surrounded.

(*Daily Chronicle* 7/11/1881)

In the lunch interval the jury were taken to view the railway carriage which had been brought near the court. A large crowd assembled to catch a glimpse of the carriage as the tarpaulin was removed. Some of the seat covers were almost ripped to pieces and there was dried blood upon the floor and splashes of blood everywhere. The jury took careful notes of the damage.

After lunch both Henry Creek, the pawnbroker who had had so much difficulty in picking out Lefroy at Cuckfield, and his assistant Ernest Allright swore that Lefroy had pawned a pistol on June 21st, before 7pm, and that he redeemed it between 11 and noon on June 27th. There was some laughter in court when Williams suggested to Creek that pawnbroking was a 'low business'. Creek indignantly replied that it was a 'high class one'.

Other pawnbrokers testified as to Lefroy's desperate straits. As each of them came forward, a fresh bundle of shabby clothes was brought into court and deposited, until the rails of the witness box presented the appearance of a pawnbroker's shop filled with articles for sale. Lefroy's clothes told a tale of grinding poverty. The court was told how first this article went for 5s and that one for 10s, how a pittance had been borrowed on an old overcoat and how a pair of trousers had been pawned for a little more. And though it might have been the flickering of the yellow gas light, Lefroy appeared to blush as one by one the evidence of his recent pauperism was held up for display.

The most controversial moment came when the prosecution called his cousin's husband, Thomas Clayton, to the witness box. He began by confirming that Lefroy had lived with them, on and off, for the last nine years. He said 'Percy' was very eccentric, especially during the week prior to the murder, and that he had not been the same since having sunstroke about a year before at Epsom Downs on Derby Day. From a child he had always been very weak and sickly, but his character was gentle, even-tempered and kind. Clayton was interrupted by the judge when he attempted to say he did not think Percy was capable of such a crime. But he did admit that he had not paid any rent for a month and was not in a position to travel First Class. He then attempted to provide an alibi for the day Lefroy had allegedly pawned the revolver:

On Tuesday 21st June I left for London at 8.45 in the morning. My wife was expecting her confinement, and was confined on the 23rd and, before I left, had complained of ill health. The prisoner in consequence volunteered to stay at home and fetch a doctor on the 21st if necessary. . . When I returned at 7.20 pm the prisoner opened the door to me.

After Sir Henry James had cross-examined Clayton, the judge intervened: 'When did you first recollect that the prisoner was at home on the 21st?''

'It has never been absent from my memory.'

'Why didn't you speak of it at the magisterial enquiry?'

'I wasn't asked.'

'Did you tell Dutton, Lefroy's solicitor?'

'No, I told no one but my wife.'

'You reserved it for the trial?'

'Yes.'

Lord Coleridge became increasingly agitated.

'You knew the importance of what you have just stated [as to his being at home on 21st June] and, as I understand, you deliberately withheld it, in order to produce it at the trial?'

'I was never asked the question.'

'You have admitted that you knew its importance; why did you not communicate it?'

The witness was silent.

'Answer the question, sir!'

The witness remained silent.

'You cannot answer it, you know you can't!'

'My lord, I cannot answer it further than I have.'

'Then you had better leave the box, sir,' said Coleridge angrily.

Thomas Clayton withdrew. Next, his wife Anne was cross-examined by the judge.

'When did the importance of the 21st first suggest itself to your mind?'

'It was some friend who first spoke to me about the 21st.'

'Who was this friend?'

'I forget. We were conversing about the case, and it was pointed out to me that the pawnbroker stated that the prisoner pawned the revolver on the 21st, and then I recollected that he was at home with me all day.'

'How long ago was this conversation?'

'About three weeks ago. It took place in my house.'

'Can you not recollect who this friend was?'

'I have tried to think, but I have forgotten.'

'Was it a man or a woman? '

'I cannot think.'

'Did you ever mention to your husband, or your husband to you, before two or three weeks ago, about his being at home on this day?'

'No.'

'Not a word passed between you and your husband on the subject?'

'No.'

'Did the prisoner ever communicate to you at all the fact that he remained at home with you on the 21st?'

'No.'

'You had no communication with him through his solicitor?'

'No, never.'

'You are perfectly confident it was the 21st he stayed at home with you?'

'Perfectly confident.'

When she stepped from the box, the judge and the counsel for the prosecution looked at each other in blank amazement. While giving their evidence, neither Claytons had looked at their relative in the dock, nor he at them.

The following day was a Sunday. Despite drizzling rain in the morning, several hundred people assembled close to the inn where the jury were lodged in the hope of seeing them go to church. Instead, the jury were escorted to the nearby prison chapel. They witnessed an impressive service conducted by the chaplain. The singing of the prisoners was particularly uplifting. A partition halfway up to the ceiling separated the male from the female prisoners, and at one point the men ceased singing and the women continued in perfect harmony.

Rather surprisingly, Lefroy was also at the service and joined in the singing. From time to time he glanced pensively at the twelve townsmen who were soon to determine whether he should live or die.

14

The Third Day.

As on previous days, the court was filled up long before proceedings were due to begin. A loud bustling noise heralded the arrival of the first witness, a rather portly woman. It was Mrs Bickers, the landlady of the house in Stepney to which Lefroy had absconded. She spoke so quietly that everyone, including the prosecution counsel, had great difficulty in hearing her replies.

The next witnesses, Swanson and Jarvis, the police inspectors who had captured Lefroy, were a vast improvement and gave their evidence concisely and clearly. Swanson described the arrest and showed the court a checked woollen shirt he had found in Lefroy's room at Stepney, nearly half of which was cut away, in order, the witness believed, to destroy the many blood stains that it contained. Swanson found small pieces that matched the shirt deeply dyed with blood, and these he held up for the inspection of the judge and jury. He also produced another item: a large false beard and moustache complete in one, which could easily be put on or off by aid of a ribbon loop. He suggested the prisoner had probably used it when he had gone out at night.

For a second time, the witness box became a sort of repository for apparel at one time belonging to the prisoner, most of it exhibiting signs of blood. A pair of tweed trousers with dried blood upon the knees, which had been worn by Lefroy on his journey to Brighton was held up and dangled before the eyes of the judge and counsel. Then Lefroy's new hat was compared with the hat he was wearing at the time of his arrest and with a hat found on the railway line, the supposition being that the last named hat might have belonged to the prisoner. The evidence about the hats proved inconclusive. Thus ended the case for the prosecution.

Minutes later Montagu Williams rose to address the jury for the defence. He had seen service in most professions, and bore the characteristics of them all. He had been an actor, and therefore carried with him a theatrical air. He had been a soldier and so displayed in his figure the jaunty elegance of an ensign in a marching regiment. He was now a most successful lawyer, and one could not fail to see in his face, accordingly, something more than the smirk of the actor, or the strut of a subaltern. He declined to call any witnesses and, standing only a yard away from the front row of the jury box, pulled his falling gown up in true Old Bailey fashion and began:

This is no ordinary case of murder, and there is no question of sanity or insanity; it is not a case in which it is likely that any mercy would be extended to the prisoner if found guilty, and therefore it is emphatically a question of life and death. It has been said that there was a 'chain' of evidence, but the jury must see that the chain was unbroken . . . otherwise the prisoner was entitled to go free. . . In this case you are being asked to embark on a sea of speculation, and I warn you against being lost and cast away upon it.

The very first link in the 'chain' of proof was wanting. Gold had retired from business and had some regular and precise habits. It was his habit every Monday to go to London to collect the week's takings and pay the money into the bank. But on the last Monday of the month it was his habit to bring down money to Preston Park along with his wife's dividends and her housekeeping money. So on that day he would probably have upon him a good sum of money and two or three sovereigns. Now, where was the evidence to show that the prisoner knew this? Is there a tittle of evidence to show that the prisoner had seen Mr Gold before in the whole of his natural life? Of course there was not. Yet this was said to be a planned murder – not a plan to murder anyone, but a plan to murder Gold. This was, however, mere theory, without any proof to affect the prisoner or connect him with it. All probability here was against the theory, and in favour of the prisoner. The theory was that he started the day with a formed plan to murder Mr Gold, and that he went from carriage to carriage looking for his victim. Where was the evidence of it, and what was the probability? Would a man, intending to commit such a murder, commit a fraud just before likely to draw attention to himself? What had he done that very morning? He had committed a petty, dirty fraud on the stationer at Croydon, getting two sovereigns in exchange for two counterfeits, thus obtaining money by false pretences, for which he could at any moment be arrested.

It was suggested, however, that he went to the railway for the purpose of committing the murder. But, surely, the probabilities were against it? Carrying in his pocket his card with right name and address; nay, more if he indeed redeemed the pistol, carrying in his pocket the pawn tickets so as to ensure his being discovered, the probabilities surely were against it. The jury would ask naturally what his story was. He admitted that he had certainly gone down to Brighton, and made an appointment to meet a young lady there, which accounted for his looking for someone and for his not being certain whether he should return, and, therefore for his taking a single ticket. What was there at all improbable in that? He was young, and it was quite natural, and it was not improbable.

Many of the articles usually carried by Mr Gold had not been found. Gold would usually have upon him two wallets and two purses; one purse had been found, the other had never been traced; one wallet had been found on the dead man's person, the other had not been found. Then there was the skull cap of Gold – where was it? If the prisoner was the man who committed the murder; where were these articles? These things were on Gold's person when he started; where were they now?

Now, let's turn to Franks, the ticket collector at London Bridge Station. He was the only witness who proved that Lefroy and Gold were in the carriage. But was he to be believed as to that? Let the jury think of the hurry and rush of that station and the work of each ticket collector in marking the tickets! Was it possible to rely on his evidence that there were only two persons in the carriage? He admitted to only seeing Lefroy for a minute and had no reason for observing him minutely, and yet professes to give a precise description of his dress! Franks said that Lefroy had a low felt hat on when it was certain he had no such hat, but a high hat. Why did he say so? Because the *Daily Telegraph* had a cut of Lefroy with such a hat on! Or if there was a third person in the carriage, then he might have had such a hat on. Franks, indeed, said that he had not seen that newspaper but could that be believed? It was a remarkable and dreadful murder, and a murder on a railway, which naturally excited public attention. Could it be supposed that he had not seen the newspaper about it. Of all the persons in the world, a person most likely to have seen it was a railway porter or ticket collector. However, such was his evidence, and that was the only witness who spoke to Gold being alone in the carriage with Lefroy.

The theory of the prosecution was that the four or five explosions heard at the entrance of Merstham Tunnel were shots, and that the bullet was then fired which penetrated Gold's neck. From that tunnel the train passed Redhill Junction, a very open and busy station, and the theory was that the bullets had then been fired, and that the two men were then engaged in their deadly struggle as the train passed through Redhill Station. Eight miles further on, at Horley, two witnesses (Mrs Brown and her daughter) spoke of seeing a struggle as the train passed. It was clear that Gold was not killed by the shot, but only momentarily stunned, so he was able to struggle. The prisoner was a weak and puny stripling; so that he would be for eight miles struggling with a tall, powerful man, and with not a particle of his dress torn, though with some wounds upon him, which he could afterwards account for.

Witnesses then saw the chain hanging out of Lefroy's boot at Preston Park. The theory was that having committed the murder he had then ransacked the body of his victim, and possessed himself of his watch and put it in his shoe, leaving the chain hanging out. But why should he do that? With a view to avoid detection in the event of a search? But if he was searched they would take his shoes off. Why did he not put the watch into his pocket? And where was the money which Gold had about him? If there was a third party in the carriage, who had taken the money and made his escape, leaving the watch behind him from fear of detection, he could easily have slipped it into the shoe of Lefroy, he then lying senseless in the carriage. What was there improbable in that? The guard stated that the train slackened to four miles an hour at Hassocks Gate and that it was possible to get from one carriage to another. Let it be remembered that the next compartment was empty; was it so when it got to Preston Park?

The prosecution had to show that there was no third man. If there was, then he could easily have got out or changed his carriage, which could easily have been done at Clayton Tunnel (four miles from Preston Park), before which every article thrown out was found. The umbrella was found at the first part of the tunnel, and had a hook on it, which would be useful in helping him escape. Or, amid the excitement at Preston Park, what was more easy than for the man to escape, assuming there was a third man in the carriage?

Then Williams alluded to Oliver Weston's evidence:

It was difficult to suppose that any man could be so wicked as to come forward to give false evidence against a prisoner on trial for his life. Yet, if the evidence of the station clerk was to be accepted as correct, then Weston's evidence was false; for the clerk said he saw no such person at the office. Was it possible that a man could have so morbid a mind as to brood and brood over a case of this character until he fancied he had had to do with it? Weston had not offered himself as a witness before the coroner or the magistrate, but came forward for the first time some weeks afterwards. Weston said he saw Lefroy outside the office, but Gibson said that he did not step outside at all, and that Weston was not there, and did not speak about 'prods of an umbrella'; that he (Gibson) would have heard the words if they were used, and that he had not heard them.

And these were both witnesses for the prosecution. What would the attorney general do or say as to Weston's evidence? If it was untrue, then a more wicked thing surely could hardly be imagined.

Now for the evidence of Holmes. Holmes knew the prisoner was wounded, and heard at Balcombe that a dead man had been found on the line; then the prisoner for the first time – if he heard it – knew of the fact, and then he must have known that he had had in his shoe the watch of the murdered man. But where were the missing purse and wallet of the murdered man, and where was the money?

Why did Lefroy flee from Wallington – the prosecution would ask – and I as his counsel ask, why did he flee? My answer is that not all men have moral courage. The prisoner had little, and he himself had said it had been better for him if he had not fled. He took to flight, however, and, though unwisely, not unnaturally. He knew he had been found in a carriage in which a murder had been committed, his person covered in blood, with the watch of the murdered man in his shoe. It was natural that he should flee, and he was weak enough to do so. There were few men who would not have fled in the circumstances. He must have fled in haste, for he left behind him the pawn tickets found in his pocket.

At one point, Williams suggested that perhaps Holmes had got Gold's watch and had hidden it away. The suggestion brought the prosecution lawyers to their feet and caused the jury to open their eyes in amazement.

Williams suited his actions to his words, raising his voice to a high pitch and then suddenly dropping the tone to a low conversational level. Arms extended, he beseeched the jury to pause before, upon doubtful evidence, they consigned the prisoner to the grave. He would point towards the prisoner when alluding to him more directly, shake the forefinger of the right hand at the jury when impressing some point upon their attention, thump the ledge with his right hand or bring one hand down upon the other with a rap that resounded through the chamber. At one time it appeared as if he was going to have musical accompaniment for the sounds of a street band playing outside floated in through the open windows, but the police quickly silenced them.

Diligent search has been made for the revolver, and it had not been found. Of course, if there was a third person who was the murderer he would have taken it away with him, and that would account for it not being found. It has been said that there were ponds and sedgy places along the line, and so there were; but surely it would require a sure aim to throw the revolver from the train into one of them. And we know that the prisoner was in a fainting state after the struggle, and if so, how could he have had the strength enough to lift the body up and throw it out?

The evidence of the pistol was of no doubt of importance; the evidence of the pawnbroker's assistants was that it was pawned on the 21st June and redeemed on the 27th, but the assistant (Creek) who spoke to the pawning, and who saw the prisoner on both occasions, would only speak to his belief, while the other assistant (Allright) swore he saw him. At all events, the pawnbroker's assistant who took the pistol on pawn would not say positively that the prisoner was the man who pawned it. There had been a portrait of the prisoner already published in the newspaper a week before he gave his evidence, and what was the value of his identification? The other assistant (Allright),was more positive, but it really was of no more value, for he was standing by the other, and if the one could not be positive neither could the other.

And to the pawning of the pistol on the 21st June, there was the evidence of Mr and Mrs Clayton that he was at home all day up to 7 o'clock. Was it to be suggested that they came here to commit perjury? The books had been produced here today, and showed that the pawning must have been before 7pm. Mr Clayton swore that he came home at twenty past seven in the evening, and that the prisoner opened the door to him. If his evidence was true, then Lefroy could not have pawned the pistol. It had been said to him (Mr Clayton), 'Did you reserve it for the trial?' and the witness, puzzled by the questions, answered 'yes' and then he was to be discredited as a witness! But he was confirmed by the simple story of his wife, who said she had asked Lefroy to stay at home that day to send for a doctor. She swore that she had her tea at 6 o'clock with Lefroy, and that he never left her until her husband returned after seven o'clock. . . Such was the whole of the evidence for the prosecution, and it was for the jury to say whether it carried conviction to their minds as an unbroken chain the links of which were perfect and complete.

It had been said that circumstantial evidence was convincing. I deny it, for it meant that human intellect was infallible. Yet how weak we are, and how open to error and mistake! Circumstantial evidence was fallible and had often misled jurors, and caused life to be sacrificed erroneously – the life of the innocent. For heaven's sake, I would say, let not this jury add another instance to the melancholy catalogue of persons so sacrificed. Let them stand and scrutinise the evidence most strictly, and bring to bear upon all the sense and judgement that God had given them. You can do but your best, but you must remember that if you err in convicting him his blood will be upon your heads, and I pray that at this awful hour He to whom all secrets are known will guide you to a rightful conclusion.

By the time Williams sat down, several of the jury were bathed in tears and one in particular wept openly. And, against all the rules, spectators broke into spontaneous applause which for a moment even the police did not attempt to stop. He had spoken for a little over three hours.

Sir Henry James, the attorney general replied for the prosecution. Such was the interest in his speech that not only was the court crowded but also the dock itself for Lefroy was hemmed in on every side by spectators who had come up the dock stairs. With some of the jury actually standing up, James began:

It was said that circumstantial evidence might mislead, and so might direct evidence; but here there was not only circumstantial evidence, there was also a great mass of direct evidence in the case, pointing, as I submit, clearly to the conclusion of guilt. There were certain facts not in dispute – the prisoner before the 27th June was in a state of need, almost desperation, pawning article after article, even of dress and clothing, even pawning the property of his friends and relatives with whom he lived. Further, it was shown that on the morning of the 27th June he was driven, in order to obtain a few shillings, to commit a fraud which was a crime.

Beyond a doubt the prisoner was with the murdered man while the murder was committed, and had upon his person marks of a struggle for life. He was also found in possession of the watch of the murdered man, and that secreted upon him. He was found then telling falsehood after falsehood about the matter. He then fled from apprehension and was found, in short, acting as a guilty man would act. Such was a general view of the evidence in the case and surely it would be sufficient to justify conviction unless he offered a reasonable explanation and defence.

James criticised the defence for suggesting – at this late stage – that Lefroy had gone to London Bridge to meet a young lady. He said the suggestion was without any evidence to support it. He then dealt with the theory of the 'third man':

The theory of the defence was that a third person, knowing Mr Gold's habits and intending to rob and murder him, proposed to do so in the presence of a third person, trusting to be able to kill him or render him insensible in the first place. Further it must be supposed that after firing at Lefroy, and after thus having aroused Mr Gold, he must have gone on to strike and disable Lefroy, and then to kill and rob Mr Gold. Was this reasonably credible? Was it within the range of credibility? But that was not all; for the third person must have proceeded to throw out the body of Mr Gold, and then gone back to the prisoner and taken his collar off and thrown it on the line. Next he must have thrown out the articles found – the purse, the hat, and umbrella – and then left behind him the gold watch, taking the trouble to put it in the prisoner's shoe. So that he must have first torn off the watch, the most valuable article on Mr Gold's person, then put it in the shoe of an insensible person. But further, this man unseen by any human eye, must have left the train somewhere, but where? No one had seen this third man. If there was, would he have taken the trouble of throwing out the prisoner's blood-stained collar? Would he have left the watch behind him in the strange way suggested?

Furthermore, the only ticket issued that day on the London to Brighton train not collected was Lefroy's. A single ticket!

Next, James described how Lefroy had been identified by the pawnbrokers over the pawning and redemption of the pistol. As for the evidence of the Claytons, he said that he only need remind the jury of the circumstances under which it was given, and if they only made a mistake in the day, or even an hour, that would account for it. He ended by reminding the jury that it would be cowardice in all of them to forget that they all had an interest in the administration of justice, and while they should be anxious not to convict the innocent, they should also be desirous that the guilty should not escape and that the public should be protected by the punishment of crime.

James sat down after speaking for two hours. His speech had been unimpassioned and judicial and his smooth-flowing sentences had contrasted strongly with the jerky, dramatic style of Williams. Nevertheless it had been full of hard, destructive facts.

Throughout the speech Lefroy sat in a dreamy listless state yawning occasionally.

That evening, Williams and James shared a train compartment back to London. James congratulated his rival: 'You have won your verdict; that fellow will be acquitted.'

'I shook my head,' recalled Williams in his book *Leaves of a Life*. 'I knew [the judge] intended to answer me on every point. "Wait till tomorrow," I said, "You've not heard the judge yet. Lefroy is a doomed man."'

Sketches from the press gallery at Maidstone assizes, published in the *Illustrated London News*, Saturday November 12, 1881.

15

The Final Day.

At daybreak, the streets surrounding the courthouse were thronged with excited crowds who had little chance of gaining admission but simply wanted to be on the spot. Later, outside the besieged building, for the last time, thousands watched the jury march two by two from the neighbouring hotel where they had been staying.

Before proceedings began, Lefroy's counsel received a dramatic telegram from Lewisham claiming that on the day of the murder a man had been admitted to a Brighton hospital with a broken leg caused by a fall from a train. Williams telegraphed to the hospital for more details. He received the following reply: *Only one patient, Albert Duckett, crushed fingers, admitted to hospital on June 27. No broken leg that day.*

Just before eleven Lefroy stepped briskly into court carrying a white handkerchief in his hand. After bowing to the judge and the jury, he sat down in his cushioned seat and giving a slight cough at once relapsed into his accustomed position of folded arms and crossed legs.

Absolute silence reigned, as the judge sifted through a huge pile of notes, and with an uplifted finger and solemn tone, began his summing up speech to the jury. His opening sentences were rendered almost inaudible by the gaol clock chiming the hour of 11 o'clock:

> Let me begin by pointing out to you the kind of persons with whom we have to deal. They are two. One is an elderly man of good means, retired from business, taking every week £30 or £40, regular in his habits, but a silent man who rather shrank from conversation with others; and went in travelling to separate himself from the others, a man of physical strength, a large man, in full health, but at the same time it is to be remembered that at his age, 64, a man's strength is not what it was. He never carried firearms. The prisoner was a person very different in all respects. He was without money, curiously erratic in his habits, not scrupulous in regard to honesty, and of his early life, how brought up, in company with what associates, we know nothing. These unfavourable circumstances I mention, not to suggest that because he would cheat he would murder, but merely to show the sort of man he was, and the temptation to which his life exposed him.

Coleridge went through the articles Lefroy had pawned in the weeks leading up to the crime:

> 30th May: an aluminium watch for 5s;
> 2nd June: an overcoat for 10s;
> 4th June: a bag with four plated spoons (marked 'R.M.O.') in it.
> 11th June: a dress suit for 15s;
> 16th June: other clothes for 15s.

The bag belonged to Mr Clayton and had been pawned without his authority. Where the spoons came from was unknown.

Coleridge continued:

Pawn tickets were found on Lefroy for all these items. These pawnings were undoubtedly by the prisoner, and the person who pawned the pistol gave the same name and address. Both the pawnbroker's assistants identified him. Against all this what is there but the evidence of the Claytons? That evidence is not merely to be set aside because they are relatives of the prisoner. Since the time of Brutus persons have sometimes told the truth even against those they loved, and their relationship of itself is not a reason for disbelieving them. But is their evidence credible? Not a word was said about it until they came here, no suggestion before the magistrates or the coroner that the murder could not have been committed by the prisoner with that pistol, because he was not near the shop on the day that it was pawned. That would have been cogent evidence for the prisoner, and it was not brought forward. Mr Clayton was a man of sense and education, and must have known the value of this piece of information, if true.

Why did he not tell it before? He knew it, he said, all along, and discussed it with his wife. She was called and gave her story about it. Asked when she first mentioned it, she said three weeks ago. So that there had been no discussion with her husband about it. She only mentioned it two to three weeks ago talking to a friend whose name she could not give. These two stories were irreconcilable. But what was the story itself? That the wife was about to be confined, and that the prisoner offered to stay at home to go for a doctor. There was a servant in the house; why could she not have gone for a doctor, or one of the pupils? And then the rest of the story was so strange, the lady keeping the school all day and going upstairs from time to time to speak to the prisoner. The hour's absence would have sufficed for the pawning. Such was the evidence to prove this alibi, and remember that the servant had no recollection of this at all.

Coleridge then referred to the folly of some of the officials on the day of the murder 'who seem to have suppressed from one another such information as might have been made use of by one or other of them'. Amidst a deep silence where even coughing, as in a church, was subdued, he vividly sketched what must have taken place during the struggle in the carriage:

Have you ever read, gentlemen, of a great work by a great author – *The Haunted House*, by Thomas Hood? In that book you will find a story of a victim who was not only caged but haunted; and that scene gives not an inadequate idea of what happened in this carriage on the London and Brighton Railway.

The terrible struggle for life – prolonged even when the victim was clinging to the footboard of the carriage – was next depicted, bringing tears to the eyes of some of the jury, and almost overcoming the widow of the deceased sitting in the narrow passage behind the dock, still clad in black. Meanwhile, Lefroy yawned again and again whilst the strongest portions of the summing-up were being delivered and did not attempt to hide the signs of his lack of interest in front of an astonished court. Coleridge briefly alluded to the fraud with the Hanoverian coins which Lefroy had carried out on the local stationer on the morning of the murder:

When he started in the carriage with Mr Gold there is strong evidence that he was in pecuniary straits, that he had a pistol and that he had some of these coins. There is no evidence to show that there was a third man in the carriage. If there was a third man, he must have been in the carriage until the Clayton tunnel was reached for there the umbrella was found thrown out, no doubt by the murderer. The defence had suggested that the third man had got out at Preston Park, but where did he go – he who had committed the murder, and must have been deluged in blood? How did he get away without being seen – covered in blood in a horrible murder?

He called the third man theory 'a mass of practical impossibilities' and attacked the defence's claim that Lefroy had gone to Brighton to meet a young lady:

Can any man believe that statement? The prisoner is on trial for his life, and it would be suicide not to call a witness who could prove a reason for a visit to Brighton. Is there an English girl who would let a man be hung rather than come forward and tell the truth? I don't believe it; do you? If not, then that again is an untruth; an untruth told at the last moment, when it is too late to disprove it. As to motives of crimes in general, they had better be left where they usually were – in obscurity. These crimes are often the result of motives that can hardly be fathomed.

Coleridge concluded:

Gentlemen, you were told by the prisoner's counsel that the evidence is all circumstantial, and that though persons have often been convicted on such evidence he does not believe in it, that it is not conclusive, and that you must not act upon it, because possibly it may be consistent with innocence. But just see what that involves. It involves that, even supposing there was no third person in the carriage, and that the prisoner did really murder Mr Gold, yet, that, as nobody saw it, and as there could be no direct proof of it, neither he nor any one would ever be convicted of it, however clear the proof might be. Gentleman, the law says nothing of the kind. The law says that in this, as in every other case, you must act on high moral probabilities.

The only difference that I am aware of between direct and circumstantial evidence is this, that direct evidence must be either believed or disbelieved, it must be either true or false; and if it is believed there is an end of the case one way, if disbelieved then there is an end of it, the other, it admits of no degrees. But we know that almost every crime in the calendar is proved day after day to the satisfaction of juries, not by direct evidence, but by evidence in its nature circumstantial. Crimes of this kind are not committed before witnesses; and if you could never prove a crime or a murder enough by direct evidence, it would almost follow that prisoners would escape and murderers would often escape justice because the evidence was circumstantial. But gentleman, there is no such rule of law.

The question is: has it been proved that this unbridled violence has been committed by the prisoner? Is it proved or not that this atrocious crime was done by him? If not, he is entitled to be acquitted; if otherwise, he must be found guilty. And, gentlemen, I trust in a case like this, where the life of a man is at issue, it is not taking the awful name of God in vain to hope that He will guide you rightly.

The judge finished his summing up in complete silence after a speech lasting more than three hours.

As the jury filed out, spectators stood up to watch them go and the hum of conversation deepened as people speculated upon the result. Disagreement over the verdict was anticipated, and even an acquittal was predicted by some. Expecting a long interval, those in the court waited for the judge to rise and for the prisoner to be taken away – but they didn't move. The judge sat quietly regarding the ceiling of the court, while the accused sat exactly opposite him, in another chair, vacantly gazing at the woodwork of the gallery.

> His pitiable appearance painfully contrasted with the lively aspect of those who talked and whispered in one great subdued chorus of expectation and speculation. 'The prisoner ought to be removed below' was on the lips of many.
>
> (*London Echo* 8/11/1881)

At one point Lefroy rose and spoke energetically over the bars of the dock to his solicitor as though suggesting something might still be urged on his behalf.

As the minutes ticked by, spectators passed the time munching sandwiches, chatting, turning over newspapers and generally wondering what they would do if there was a long wait, when, to the astonishment of everyone, a cry for 'silence in court' rang out. The change from noise to complete quietness seemed electrical in its suddenness.

Then a sound at the back of the court caused all eyes to turn in the direction of the jury box where, emerging from behind a crimson curtain, the foreman was seen leading the way into court for his colleagues. They had been gone only ten minutes.

16

As one by one the jury stepped into the box and took their seats, eager faces strained round pillars and corners to catch sight of their demeanour. They saw immediately that the prisoner's doom seemed to be depicted in each one of their countenances. One aged juror hid his face with his handkerchief, another gave way to tears and one man at the end of the box, trembling with emotion, had to grasp a gas bracket in order to support himself.

When the foreman pronounced the verdict 'Guilty', a deep woman's wail broke the awful silence. Then came a peremptory call for the prisoner to 'Stand up!' Lefroy unfolded his arms and sprang to his feet.

'Have you anything to say why sentence of death should not be pronounced upon you?' asked the clerk.

Placing his hands on the rail of the dock, Lefroy, in a hoarse, hardly audible voice, replied, 'I have only to thank the gentlemen of the jury . . .'

This was all he was allowed to utter, for at this point the old-fashioned cry for 'Silence in court' rang out and a warder placed his hand on the prisoner's shoulder. Stopped in what he was going to say, Lefroy once more put his hands behind his back and straightened himself up.

Throughout the whole of this memorable trial one dreadful object has ever and anon appeared in view. On the first day of the case – as far back as Friday – it could be seen, nestled snugly under the leg of the desk at which the Lord Chief Justice sat, partially hidden too by the lavender gloves of his lordship and now almost disappearing from view as the books with which the Judge dealt were pushed hither and thither. Then it came nearer, and was presently to be found, not placed against the woodwork as before, but between the notebook which his lordship had filled and the one on which he was writing – still nearer, yesterday getting under his lordship's elbow, till this morning it was to be seen mixed up with his papers on which the Judge had made the notes for his speech.

From there but one more movement was possible; it must either disappear altogether, or be placed upon his lordship's head. And it was there – the black cap – that I saw it, when, on glancing from the pallid prisoner in the dock to the flushed jury in the box at a quarter to three this afternoon, I turned to hear the Lord Chief Justice of England pronounce sentence of death upon Percy Lefroy

Mapleton. Dismal indeed was the scene which at that moment presented itself.

(*Daily Telegraph* 9/11/1881)

The judge bowed his head low:

Percy Lefroy Mapleton, you have been convicted on the clearest evidence of an atrocious murder – a murder perpetrated with knives and firearms, on an old, harmless man who had done you no harm; you have been rightly convicted, and it is only fair that you should be.

I will not harrow your feelings or endanger my self-command by going into the facts of the murder, or by attempting to estimate your moral character. He who knows temptation can estimate your sin; it is not for the sin of your crime that the law punishes you. The law punishes your crime. Your sins whatever they may be will be judged hereafter.

The sentence of the court upon you is that you be taken from hence to the place whence you came, and from thence to the proper place of execution, and that you be hanged there by the neck until you are dead. May God have mercy upon your soul.

Some of the jurors cried 'Amen'.

Lefroy advanced to the iron rails. Suddenly he grasped convulsively at them and swayed to and fro, as though about to fall. But he soon regained control and, folding his arms, he stared at the jury intently. Just before he left the dock, with a warder holding him by the shoulder, he turned theatrically towards them and said gravely: 'Gentlemen of the jury, some day when too late, you will learn that you have murdered me.'

He was quickly removed from the dock and taken down below. On reaching the cells he asked for a cup of tea, which he drank with obvious relish. He was manacled. He was now a convict.

Amid chaotic scenes, Lefroy was quickly despatched to the railway station and started the slow journey back to Lewes. As the train passed stations packed with excited crowds, he constantly saw his name on posters with the verdict printed in large letters underneath.

Numerous newspapermen followed Lefroy all the way from the courthouse right up to the gates of Lewes Prison. By the time the police pushed him through the small wicket door in the entrance a crowd had gathered and he could hear them jeering and shouting at him.

On his arrival he was taken to a double sized cell in the basement – the 'condemned cell' – where the warders made him change into coarse prison clothing with its distinguishing broad arrow marks. The cell was situated in the north-east wing, 50 yards from the 'execution' yard.

The Press showed little surprise at the verdict:

The trial of Percy Lefroy Mapleton, alias Arthur Lefroy, for the murder of Isaac Gold terminated in the only way it could have expected to terminate. A case hopeless from the very first.
(*The Times* 10/11/1881)

Fewer clearer cases ever came before a court of justice.
(*Daily News* 10/11/1881)

It is impossible to see what other verdict could have been pronounced.
(*The Standard* 10/11/1881)

One of the most astonishingly cruel and cold-blooded assassinations of modern times has thus been traced to its undoubted source. Mercy in such a case is out of the question. The worst feature of this atrocious crime is its character of cool calculation. The assassin was not mad, unless every criminal is to be regarded from the mere fact of the crime as suffering from cerebral disease. Nevertheless, we may safely comfort ourselves with the thought that such a character only appears once or twice in a generation, and is altogether abnormal. There need be no public panic about our railway carriages becoming the lurking places of the secret assassin.
(*The Daily Telegraph* 10/11/1881)

Most of the post-trial newspaper reports speculated on the motive for the crime. Nearly all attributed it to the greed for money, as did the sermons in Maidstone the following Sunday. But one touched on an altogether different explanation:

If I might here interject a bit of irresponsible gossip, it would be in the direction of repeating the rumour that the guiding motive in Lefroy's career has been the love of a pretty woman – that everything he is alleged to have done has been with the purpose of enabling him to stand well, in a monetary sense, with a certain, or perhaps uncertain lady. The impassive countenance, however, that faces me as I write, betrays no tale of love or romance.
(*West Sussex Gazette* 10/11/1881)

17

Lefroy's execution was fixed to take place at nine o'clock at Lewes Prison on Tuesday, 29th November, three weeks after the end of the trial. Selected journalists were to be allowed in as witnesses in the hope (of the authorities) that their reports might act as a deterrent.

On the penultimate day of the trial, Lefroy's family had asked an eminent psychiatrist, Dr. L.S. Forbes-Winslow, to attend and study his mental state in the Maidstone courtroom. Shortly afterwards, he wrote a letter to a national newspaper, a letter which started a public debate:

> I must confess that I was surprised that the question of the responsibility of the prisoner was not raised. There is no doubt that Lefroy has a strong hereditary predisposition to insanity, his father and grandfather having both been insane. His behaviour in Court was a most strange and unnatural one, the explanation to me being either that he was indifferent to what was going on, or that he was for some reason, not yet explained, unaware of the gravity of his position.
>
> (*Daily News* 10/11/1881)

In fact, Lefroy had been so confident of an acquittal he had allegedly told one of his gaolers: 'When I am acquitted, I hope I shan't be mobbed.' It was also rumoured that he had written to one of his sisters asking her to get a cab ready for when he was released. His behaviour at his trial even astonished his own lawyer, Montagu Williams.

> Before the attorney general commenced his speech, the prisoner placed his hat on a ledge at the side of the dock. He took it up again, and then once more returned it to the ledge. Apparently he was loath to part with it.
>
> Every morning, on taking his place in the dock, he put his hat down with the greatest circumspection, in the exact spot that he had originally selected for it . . . On the second day, the Police Superintendent of Lewes gave evidence.
>
> 'He asked me,' said the superintendent, 'to let him have the pawn ticket for his evening dress, as he wished to appear in it at his trial.' The persons, in court smiled, and no wonder. The picture presented to the mind, of the prisoner, arrayed in evening dress,

standing behind the spiked bars of the dock, was irresistibly ludicrous. . . Perhaps in his mind evening clothes denoted extraordinary respectability. Of all his worldly goods, they were certainly the last he parted with; and of all his wardrobe, they were in the best condition. When he did pawn them, it was only under pressure of absolute want. He was, in a word, a man steeped in a kind of petty, strutting, theatrical vanity. Nevertheless, it was almost inexplicable that he should devote more attention to his hat than to the proceedings of the trial.

It was curious to note the change that took place in Lefroy's bearing and demeanour whenever he caught sight of an artist from one of the illustrated papers in the act of sketching him. He suddenly brightened up, and, if I am not mistaken, assumed a studied pose for the occasion.

Lefroy's solicitor, Dutton, began to prepare a petition to the Home Office, asking for a reprieve on the grounds of insanity. But one man was against it; Lefroy himself. In prison he was still maintaining his innocence and claiming that there was a 'third man' whose discovery would explain everything. He remained calm and unemotional. The prison chaplain, Rev. Thomas Cole, informed Anne Clayton that 'the way he received his ministrations left nothing to be desired in the way of gentleness and submission.' On November 12th, she wrote to several national newspapers:

Dear Sirs.

With a heart almost breaking, with an agony too great for words, I write to entreat space in your columns for a few words on the subject of my unhappy but tenderly loved cousin, Percy Lefroy Mapleton. Almost every newspaper has teemed with accounts of his errors and crimes until the public can scarcely help believing that to his character and disposition there is not – what is generally allowed to all others – an 'angel side'.

How bitter this is to those who love him can be imagined, and all I seek to do is to state in a few words what his home life and disposition have been during all his twenty-one years. From quite a child reading had been his favourite amusement, both his natural temperament and delicacy of constitution rendering more active pastimes undesirable. Gentle, even-tempered, and affectionate, he has always been truly loved by his immediate family, and from his having lived ever since his birth with me, no one is better able to speak so of him. I can honestly assert that in his whole life I have never known him to harm an animal or speak angrily to a living soul, although his extraordinary delusions were always a source of distress to us. My little children love him dearly, and have always looked to him for amusement and enjoyment; while to me, he has been as a kind and attentive brother. Only this time last year he was a patient nurse to my aged and dying mother, and to believe him capable of the frightful deed imputed to him is to us, who know him so well, an utter impossibility. Losing him at all would be an intense grief, but to lose him in this most awful of all awful ways means home desolation and misery, which can end only with our lives.

The letter provoked considerable surprise and some sympathy, even from the Brighton press:

The lady . . . at a period when disgrace so heavily hangs upon her family, does not hesitate to come forward not merely with an acknowledgement – a public pronouncement – of her cousinship to a convicted murderer, but with assertions respecting an intimacy and affection for the prisoner far beyond what cousins generally entertain.

Under ordinary circumstances, it might be assumed that a woman so sensible of the disgrace such a connection involved might have been expected to have held her peace, and rather to have microfied than magnified her relationship. Mrs Clayton, however, has made no such attempt, and nothing tends so much as this one fact to give importance to her communication, and to afford an evidence of her own conviction of the truth of her statements.

Under these circumstances we shall be surprised if many people do not feel that the question of Lefroy's moral responsibility is more open to reasonable discussion than was supposed whilst public horror was at its height, owing to the magnitude of the crime and the cunning with which it was committed.

(*Brighton Evening Argus* 15/11/1881)

Lefroy's local newspaper, the *Croydon Guardian* (12/11/1881), raised another concern:

No man had been so prejudged as was Arthur Lefroy. The result of the trial justified the opinion formed, but it is adverse to a man's chance to be on trial by the public for months before a judge.

On November 15th it was widely reported that the home secretary, William Harcourt, after receiving numerous letters about Lefroy, had decided to send an eminent medical man to Lewes to examine and report on his mental state. But it was a false report, quickly denied the following day. Dutton then wrote to Harcourt, asking him to give permission for Forbes-Winslow and another doctor, J.M. Winn, to visit Lefroy. His request was refused.

A few days later, with the family's agreement, Dutton presented the following petition to the home secretary:

1. That the evidence entirely failed to show the slightest premeditation, and that there is the strongest possible ground for believing that the act was done under the influence of homicidal mania, there being, as will be subsequently disclosed, a great predisposition to insanity from the family history of the accused.
2. That the defence set up at the trial would have been that the accused was not responsible for his acts by reason of the state of his mind, had not his solicitor, Mr Dutton, who acted for him throughout, received positive directions from the accused as to the presence of a third person in the carriage, which neither his solicitor nor his relatives were of course, in a position to disregard.
3. That the father of the accused died of softening of the brain [a euphemism for senility].
4. That his grandfather also became insane some time prior to his death.
5. That his uncle was also insane, and actually died in a lunatic asylum.
6. That the accused himself, who has always been of a weak, sickly temperament, had a sunstroke whilst standing on the racecourse at Epsom on Derby Day of 1880, on which occasion he fell down in a fit and was taken home in a conveyance and confined to his bed for several days, and has never been the same man, having been subjected to long and continued fits of despondency and depression.
7. That the demeanour of the accused during the continuance of the trial was one of stolid indifference, and that he seemed in no way, either before or after his sentence, to realise the gravity of his situation, we, your petitioners, attribute to the distressed condition of his mind.

Your petitioners, therefore, humbly pray that a competent medical enquiry may forthwith be made into the mental condition of the above named Percy Lefroy Mapleton; and that should, as your petitioners anticipate, a report be made that he is not, and has not been for some time responsible for his actions, her most gracious Majesty be advised mercifully to reprieve the sentence of death passed upon him; and your petitioners, as in duty bound, will ever pray.

It was signed by almost 2,000 people, including doctors, clergymen and members of the aristocracy. Attached to it was evidence from the family's doctor, Thomas Green. He had treated Lefroy's mother at the time of his birth and found her to be suffering from 'intense melancholia and paroxyms of frenzy' and he believed that the taint of insanity was likely to become hereditary. Green had known Lefroy since he was a young boy and remembered him being physically weak and suffering from hereditary lung disease. Green had also treated Lefroy's father whom he described as insane as a result of excessive drinking. An uncle, Captain George V. Seale, claimed that one of Captain Mapleton's commanding officers 'begged the friends of that mad Mapleton' to ask him to resign his appointment as magistrate at St Helena to prevent him from being dismissed. Another officer wrote that on one occasion Mapleton had tried to smother his wife and commit suicide.

Another doctor had seen Lefroy two years before and had noted that 'this man is insane'. In addition, Forbes-Winslow had interviewed some of the crew who had been on Lefroy's return journey from Australia. They told him Lefroy had acted so strangely that they had had to put him under 'absolute restraint'.

Evidence of the goodness of Lefroy's family was also sent to the Home Office. George Seale described Lefroy's younger sister Julia, who was a matron at the fever hospital in Liverpool Street, Islington:

At the time of the Russo-Turkish war she offered her services as a nurse for the sick and wounded and went out to Bulgaria. Whilst there she nursed many Russian soldiers who were ill with fever and in consequence caught a severe attack of typhoid fever herself and was so ill that for some time her life was despaired of.

Anne Clayton also sent the Home Office a letter which she had just received from the woman who had been Lefroy's landlady at Ventnor four years before:

18th November 1881
Dear Mrs Clayton,
    You will remember me when I tell you Mr Mapleton, or Lefroy, as he is now called, lodged with me a whole winter four years ago,

and I must say a better-conducted or more gentlemanly young man I never had in my house; but sometime before he left I found him very strange, and I believe him subject to hallucinations, for after he had been out for a walk, he would tell me of people he had met which he could not possibly have seen, as they were not in Ventnor at the time. He also said he had received threatening letters, which was not true, and I cannot tell you of all the strange things he said and did in this letter. However, he said he must leave Ventnor, for there was a man following him about wherever he went.

I am very sorry for him about his predicament, but I don't think at all times he is responsible for his actions. I would have written to him before, but I saw from the newspapers that he would not allow his solicitor to plead insanity; but it is my belief he is insane.

Please accept all my sympathy, and believe me to be, yours truly, A. Dodds.

P.S. You can make whatever use you like of this letter.

With growing public concern about a possible miscarriage of justice, a protest meeting was organised on Clerkenwell Green, London. On November 14th, shortly before midnight, an argument broke out over Lefroy's guilt at a public house in Bethnal Green. John Beedham and James Newman started to fight and were asked to leave. They then, in the company of friends, went to a local park, took off their coats and resumed the contest. By the end of the evening, Beedham was dead and Newman had disappeared. Two days later, he was arrested and charged with manslaughter.

Back in Wallington, groups of ladies organised a door to door petition asking for a reprieve, and Mrs Clayton told the press she was receiving numerous expressions of sympathy and offers of assistance. She also received an anonymous letter with a London postmark. It was in a lady's handwriting and stated that she had been due to meet Lefroy at London Bridge Station on the day of the murder. The family passed the letter to Dutton.

Other letters, from 'One Who Knew Lefroy', began to appear in the *Daily Telegraph*:

There is no doubt that Lefroy possessed a wonderful knack of making falsehoods appear as truth but . . . he preferred to figure as a benefactor rather than one who benefits. . . .I think it will be seen from first to last Lefroy never contrived matters to be himself a gainer. In the theatrical speculations which, I believe, indirectly led to his withdrawal to Australia, he appears to have overlooked his own interests, for I have been assured that he could not possibly have handled any money and escaped. At Wallington he took upon himself the getting up of a cricket match and here again he saddled himself with the expenses.

Later on – and of this I have personal knowledge – he arranged another cricket match, refused to let his side contribute to his expenses and then allegedly cut some of their bags and extracted money to pay the bill. Moreover, looking at the character of his schemes – the daring with which they were presented, and the almost certainty of the detection of the fraud – inclines me to a belief that they were due to some phase of mind which cannot be termed a sane condition. This impression, coupled with the recollection of his gentle manner, his absence of excitement upon any occasion, his complete self-control, the kindly consideration he was ever disposed to show to others, and the courtesy apparently inborn and not acquired, which characterised him, weigh considerably with me.

With a little more than a week to go before the execution, another of Lefroy's local newspapers, the *Croydon Chronicle* (19/11/1881), detected a change in public mood:

In London circles there is a considerable change of opinion as to what ought to be done with Lefroy. Last week with the details of the tragedy re-opened by the evidence of the trial, there was a very large majority in hanging the poor wretch off hand. But Mr Forbes-Winslow's letter set people thinking, and now it is generally conceded that the wretched man should not be hanged until the state of his mind is thoroughly investigated.

Lefroy's deception of his solicitor seems proof of his insanity. He was constantly leading him astray by the most absurd statements, and sending him all over the country to get evidence from people who did not exist, or had never heard of Lefroy before the murder. In the interest of humanity, it is hoped that the prisoner will not be hanged unless it can be shown that he really is sane.

That afternoon, it was reported that a man walked into a waxworks museum in Brighton, and, with a hammer, destroyed a model of Frederick Gold. A model of Lefroy next to it remained untouched.

18

On November 19th Lewes Prison echoed to a chilling sound. It came from one of the exercise yards. It was the noise of hammers on wood and metal. The works unit had started to construct the gallows which would put an end to Lefroy. On the same day a man in Barnstable walked into the local police station and confessed to the murder of Gold. He said his name was Robert Flak and that he was a chemist. He claimed to know the prison chaplain, Thomas Cole, whom he had met whilst in Lewes for stealing shirts in Brighton. Cole had never heard of him. Flak was discovered to be drunk and the police put him in Exeter Gaol as they thought he might be wanted for some other crime.

Meanwhile, Lefroy was receiving many hundreds of tracts and religious publications asking him to confess. Some he was refusing to even look at, with the agreement of Thomas Cole. He spent most of his time writing letters to his friends and family. In one, he asked Anne Clayton if he could see her eldest child Melville, aged seven, for one last time. In another he wrote lovingly to Frank Seale, the cousin with whom he had shared a bedroom at their house in Wallington:

My dearest Frank,
How to write to you I scarcely know. It seems but yesterday that as a baby child I was taking your dear kindly hand and rambling with you by the dear old Surrey hills, plucking the flowers as I passed. It seems but yesterday that I, still but a fragile child, was standing clothed in gloomy mourning by your side at an open grave, watching with frightened curiosity the last sad interment of my own dear mother.

All the past years from childhood to youth, from youth to manhood, this last attained but nine months ago, are marked as some long weary road might be with milestones, and on each stone I see, even in this sad, memory-haunted place, but one inscription, 'A cousin's sacrifice, a cousin's love'. When I look back through the vista of years, and think of the thousand and one proofs of your love I have had, and have never requested, I wonder sincerely why God has not punished me for my vile ingratitude to you long, long ago.

But the past is gone – that, at all events, can never be re-called. But the future – the glorious future – is by God's mercy in our own hands. I may – nay, I shall – die an ignominious death in the eyes of what is called the world, and your earthly life may for the future be dull and cheerless, though God knows I hope this last may not be so. But when both our short lives on earth are ended, what a glorious, nay, even an awful thought – through its grandeur – that you and I, together with all we love, may meet once more, never to part again.

Oh, my darling, God knows I have no right to speak like this to you, but I cannot, cannot help it. Until I came here this last time I had never properly understood what this meant – this wonderful promise of future life – but now, when my days are numbered, and the shadow – rather, I should say the glorious light – of death is falling softly on me, I seem to see it. Perhaps without this awful chastening I might never in the ordinary course of life have seen it at all until too late; and if this, indeed, be so, I thank God Almighty for His goodness in letting me be as I now am, rather than a free man, exposed to all the temptations and trials of this world.

Hope on, my dearest brother, nay, rather pray on. Give all the loving words and deeds you can to darling Anne, who, God knows, will need them. Do your duty on earth as you always have done it – bravely and fearlessly, and imitate as far as you can the life of my long lost, but much loved, mother. With God's help you can do all this, and more. And then, dearest, when your life is as nearly closed as mine is, you will feel such peace of mind, such rest, as you never felt before. That you may feel this shall be one of my last prayer's to God.

Yours ever, 'Percy'.

Frank Seale went to visit him in prison. The visiting room was divided in the middle from floor to roof by a double row of stout iron bars with a 3ft wide passage-way between them. Lefroy was placed between the innermost bars; the deputy-governor sat in the passageway while Seale was placed on the outside.

On seeing his cousin, Lefroy brightened up considerably. Leaning against the bars he told him he was expecting the worst and to give his love to his family. Seale replied that they had been inundated with letters and suggestions about the case and hardly knew what to do with them all. Lefroy smiled and apologised for the trouble he had caused. He said he was grateful for their exertions in trying to get him a reprieve but he was innocent, not mad. Seale replied that he had always believed him and had never doubted that he was telling the truth. Lefroy told him he was being treated well by the prison staff.

The meeting lasted about twenty minutes and the cousins separated without being allowed to shake hands.

The following day Seale visited him again with Anne Clayton. This time Lefroy was allowed to sit in the passageway – a concession on the part of the governor, Captain Crickett, to Mrs Clayton who wanted to shake his hand. Lefroy was overjoyed to see them, although he expressed great disappointment at the absence of Melville. His cousin said she would try to bring him tomorrow. This cheered him up. He said he would not like to die without kissing his 'little companion' goodbye. He told them he was fully prepared to meet his fate and had given up any ideas of a reprieve.

He turned to Frank Seale – as this was to be their last farewell – and spoke about their lifelong friendship: 'Frank, you have been more than a cousin to me, you have been father and brother in one.' He thanked him again and again for his care and tenderness over his childhood, youth and manhood. He referred to their many pleasant rambles and studies together, and smiled several times as he alluded to various incidents.

After nearly an hour, Lefroy said goodbye to Anne Clayton and, shaking her hands, kissed her through the bars. He then turned to Frank Seale. Pressing his face desperately against the bars, he put both his hands through and clasping his cousin sobbed aloud. Both remained for a few minutes tightly clasping each other's hands. 'Farewell' was said again and again, and at the last goodbye Lefroy kissed Seale and with a great effort they parted.

On their way out, the chaplain, Thomas Cole, spoke to the cousins. He said that Lefroy had endeared himself to all the prison officials on account of his 'gentleness and quiet demeanour'. He also told them something else – that for the last two days Lefroy had been feverishly writing away but had refused to let anyone see what he was writing.

Thursday 24th November
As the campaign to obtain a reprieve reached its height, supportive letters were printed in the medical journal, the *Lancet*, and in many national newspapers. His family sent one of them to the home secretary:

It is with great regret I learn from the daily papers that the home secretary has determined to let the law take its course, without giving the prisoner the benefit of a mental examination by an experienced expert. The facts in support of the plea of insanity are very strong. From a careful consideration of the case, and perusal of certain documents now in possession of Dr Forbes Winslow, and not made public (written before the murder and since his condemnation, facts which can only possibly be known to those who have perused them; data affording invaluable aid in conducting an examination of the prisoner), I am of the opinion that competent and experienced experts should have been allowed to examine the unhappy prisoner.

Your obedient servant,
J.M. Winn, M.D. Harley Street.

Another respected medical man also made a public appeal:

I heartily and anxiously endorse Dr Winn's opinion that Lefroy should be examined by competent experts. It is indeed to be regretted that the obstinacy of the prisoner could not have been overruled, and the plea of insanity substituted for the 'third' person theory advocated by the defence. It is well known that this was the desire of his relatives. I have before me now a letter written a few days ago by one of his sisters, in which she writes, 'Whatever the public may think, I am sure my poor young brother was not in his right mind, for when I saw him for the first time after an interval of eighteen months, I was very unhappy about his looks and manner, and wrote the next day to his friends about him, and it was my earnest wish that the defence should have been he was insane. There were so many things about him that made us unhappy. I was struck by it when I saw him, and bitterly regret now that I did not call medical advice for him. He was naturally too loving and gentle to have done anything cruel if he had not been out of his mind; but it is too late now, I am afraid.'

But I do trust, sir, that it is not too late, though it be the eleventh hour, for such an examination of the condemned man's mental condition to be made. . . The law may be vindicated and society protected by the execution of a responsible murderer, but justice is outraged and society imperilled by the hanging of a lunatic. Which is Lefroy?

Your obedient servant,
William Henry Netherclift Med.Sup. of the Chelsea Infirmary.

On the same day an MP, J. Stansfield, received a visit from a leading feminist, Miss Lucy Wilson from Chelsea, asking him to arrange a meeting with the home secretary. Impressed by her sharp mind, he tried to arrange one. It was refused, but Harcourt did agree to read any letter she might wish to send him. Lucy Wilson personally delivered the following letter:

The Treasury never offered the reward for the murder but for the capture of Lefroy. This created a strong impression that he was guilty and discouraged an enquiry as to any other possible culprit. The extreme rapidity with which the jury came to a conclusion on the very imperfect and contradictory evidence put before them, suggests that they had not been able to entirely clear their minds of the impression that they, in all probability shared with others. The judge, from the beginning to the end of the trial, constituted himself counsel for the prosecution. He severely and angrily censured the Claytons for giving evidence in favour of the prisoner which they had not given at the preliminary enquiry, and he uttered no word of rebuke or comment to Mr Weston when he did precisely the same thing against the prisoner. His summing up was a more hostile edition of the attorney general's reply; he never once put, as he was bound to do, the theory of the prisoner's innocence before the jury and showed how far the facts were consistent with that. It is not possible that his exhibition of a strong conviction on his part, could fail to bear weight with the jury.

A few years ago no one would have dreamed of convicting a man on a capital charge on such evidence as was put before the jury. He did not establish any motive apart from poverty but he had been poorer before without killing anybody. He took no money and was unlikely to get much on such a train. Where was the knife? Where was the pistol? Somebody could have known Mr Gold's habits. The bloody fingerprints on the train footboard could have been the victim or the escaping murderer. The presence of a third person in the carriage and his escape from it would account for everything that occurred, and nothing else would. Lefroy's injuries were the result of attempts to get rid of a weak and awkward witness.

The fact that the prisoner spent four hours in company with policemen and railway servants in Brighton, underwent repeated questioning and was searched, and finally travelled back with a policeman over the scene of the morning's deadly struggle and crime, without his demeanour once raising a suspicion of guilt in the trained minds of his companions, affords strong presumption of his innocence.

Lefroy was dressed in a light overcoat (it would show every speck and stain of blood), killed him, threw money out of the window, which he might have kept without any present danger; kept his watch, the most dangerous thing he could keep; put it in the most conspicuous place and called up the people at the station to observe his bloodstained condition and that of the carriage and to see the watch in his shoes. He remained in, to him, the most dangerous company for four hours without showing any unease or attempting to get away, gave his real address, kept the watch after it had been seen and examined and understandably claimed it and told falsehoods about his possession of it at the moment when it was most dangerous to do so. His calm and unmoved bearing that day was that of either an innocent man, a hardened and practical criminal, or a madman. It is denied that he was the first, it is not pretended that he was the second, there remains only the last.

The facts of his hereditary predisposition to insanity, of his own mental weakness, of his extraordinary delusions and his living in dreams of his own creating and constantly asserting to be facts things which have not existence but in his own imagination, have, I understood, been brought to your knowledge in a memorial prepared by his family. I will not refer to them further than to point out that the false statements which he made on the day of the murder and which undoubtedly and not unnaturally created considerable prejudice against him, are thus proved to lose their significance and to be not inventions at the moment of a guilty man seeking to escape detention, but the constant habit of his life.

Later that day, with the waxworks model of Lefroy already being made for the Madame Tussauds executioners gallery in London, Mr and Mrs Clayton and their son Melville paid a farewell visit. Lefroy, in the presence of the deputy-governor, was allowed to see the child in his cell for 10 minutes. On the boy's entry, Lefroy caught him in his arms, thanked him for coming and kissed him again and again. The boy presented him with some flowers which he had brought from Wallington. Taking Melville on his knee, Lefroy tenderly caressed him, and talked about his little brother and sister, and told him to tell them to be good and not to forget him. On parting, he took Melville in his arms and kissed him and then was taken by two warders to the visitor's room.

He asked Mrs Clayton to thank all those people who had written letters of sympathy to him and who had subscribed to the fund to defray the expense of his defence. This, he said, he wished done in addition to the letters of thanks he had already written himself. Next, he talked about the disposal of his possessions. He wanted his little companion, Melville, to have his writing desk and that the few things he had in prison be given to his two sisters.

He finished by saying they would meet before long and not to dread the parting any more than when he had left for Australia. After saying their final goodbyes the Claytons left the prison in tears.

Next Lefroy saw his solicitor, Dutton, who informed him that he had received no news from the Home Office. The precise nature of their conversation was unclear, but after the solicitor had gone Lefroy became agitated. That night the warders claimed he walked up and down in his cell like a madman, 'gesticulating, moaning and raving in a dreadful manner.'

First thing the next morning, Lefroy rang the bell for his gaoler and asked to see the chaplain. He said he had something very important to tell him.

19

Saturday 26th November.

Cole hurried along to Lefroy's cell. What he heard took him completely by surprise. Lefroy confessed to the unsolved murder of a Lieutenant Roper of the Royal Engineers who had been shot earlier in the year at Chatham Barracks on February 11th. Lefroy claimed that he had shot him for insulting a famous young actress he called 'May Gordon' and who he deeply loved. He still denied murdering Mr Gold. The chaplain reported the conversation to the governor, who immediately sent him to London to inform the Home Office.

In the afternoon, Lefroy's older sister, Mary Brickwood, visited him for the last time. He told her, 'I do not know what has been the matter with me all the while; I sometimes think I must have been two persons.' He then repeated the confession he had made to the chaplain. She kissed him several times before leaving.

Afterwards the governor told her that Lefroy had 'rushed about his cell like a raging lion' all night, and that he himself had stayed up and watched him.

Dutton wrote the following letter to the home secretary:

Dear Sir,
I had an interview with the convict Lefroy on Friday, and from what transpired then, and has been communicated to me since from those who had later interviews with him, I am convinced in my own mind that the murder of Lieutenant Roper was the act of the man now lying under sentence of death. He has admitted the fact both to his sister and the chaplain of the gaol.

The object of this letter is to beg you to grant me an immediate interview that I may more fully explain what has transpired, and in the interest of public justice must press upon you the necessity of a respite in order to make the necessary investigation. The statements made as to the Chatham murder and other matters which have come to my knowledge convince me that this unhappy man is the victim of homicidal mania. I have the honour to be your humble and obedient servant. . .

In an interview, Dutton told journalists that 'no one could be 10 minutes in Lefroy's company without questioning his sanity. He is and probably has been for three or four years past, undoubtedly insane – what, for want of a better word, I should call a "blood man"'.

In late newspaper editions, the following letter appeared:

Dear Sir,

Permit me to endorse this appeal for a delay. The plea is not for pardon but for postponement. Time is required for investigation. Innocent persons have been suspected of the murder of Lieutenant Roper, and it was even suggested that he might have committed suicide. If the confession now made by Lefroy is verified, these cruel suspicions will be wiped away, and the friends of the murdered officer relieved from a painful stigma. Besides, there may be more to confess; who knows how much more light there may be to throw over the career of this homicidal maniac during the past three years?

A few more days more or less can be of little consequence to the condemned man at Lewes, but justice demands that if he be really of unsound mind he should not be hanged, and at any rate a brief space should be allowed for the detective department to follow up the clues he has given them before he is placed irrevocably beyond the reach of examination or confession as well as beyond the prerogative of mercy.

Yours truly, ONE WHO KNOWS LEFROY

The Home Office decided to send Superintendent Coppinger of the Chatham police to Lewes Prison to investigate the matter. There it was reported that Lefroy was in such a weak state he had to be helped back to his cell after taking exercise in the courtyard. After a lengthy interview with Lefroy, Coppinger reported to his superiors that he did not believe he had anything to do with Roper's death.

Speculation about the identity of 'May Gordon' now became rife in the Press. In his book, *Suspicion Aroused* (1893), Dick Donovan gave details about one actress in Lefroy's life:

As near as the time can be fixed, it was about two years before the commission of the deed that Lefroy made the acquaintance of an exceedingly pretty girl, who occupied a humble position as an actress at a London theatre. How he first made the girl's acquaintance is not clear. She knew him by the name of Arthur Henry Nelson, and he had the impudence to claim descent from the famous Lord Nelson, and gave her to understand that he was entitled to a large amount of property on the death of an uncle, who was then eighty years of age. The girl was foolish enough to believe all this, and when after they had known each other some little time he asked her to become his wife she gladly consented, subject to his introducing her to his relatives and family. This he promised to do, but subsequently he told her that he was sure if his uncle came to hear that he had associated with an actress the fortune would be willed away elsewhere, for the old gentleman had a strong dislike to the stage and to all connected with it.

The plausibility of Lefroy's story led the girl to believe that it was true, but when he urged her to marry him secretly, and vow on the Bible not to disclose the secret until he gave her permission to do so, she flatly and indignantly refused, saying that if his friends did not choose to recognise her openly the connection must cease, for she would not consent to any secrecy.

This angered him very much, and, as she was inflexible, he gave her up, notwithstanding that she had from time to time lent him sums of money, amounting in the aggregate to several pounds.

But this lady was not 'May Gordon'. Neither was she the woman who had sent Lefroy a letter – containing stamps – to Mrs Bicker's house which arrived the day after he had been arrested. She was never traced.

The real identity of the woman whom it was rumoured Lefroy was obsessed with was revealed by the lady herself in a letter to all the major newspapers the day after the Roper confession. She was, in fact, one of the most famous young actresses of the day.

As my name has been most unfortunately mixed up with the case of Lefroy, I beg that you will give an emphatic denial to the report that he was at any time known to me. I never saw him or exchanged a word with him in my life. But since his conviction he has written me a most painful and unaccountable letter which is now in the possession of Dr Forbes Winslow.

Yours sincerely, Violet Cameron.

Born on 7th December 1862, Violet Cameron was the cousin of the actresses Violet and Florrie Lloyd, and had first appeared on stage at the age of seven and had been touring since she was 12. At the time of Lefroy's trial, although only 18, she was at the height of her popularity. In September of that year she was starring as Bettina in *La Mascotte* (The Luck-Bringer) at the Theatre Royal, Brighton – the theatre owned by Mrs Nye Chart. *The Stage* described her performance:

Violet Cameron could not look prettier nor sing more saucily as the fair rustic beauty. She is one of the prettiest, most graceful and accomplished of our actresses, and one of the most charming songstresses of the day.

At the beginning of October the show transferred to the Comedy Theatre, London, and the Prince of Wales attended the first night. Her co-star was Henry Bracy. In the week the trial started she married a Mr David de Bensuade. Once her name had been linked with Lefroy the newspapers published stories about his obsession for her.

He used to represent to his relatives, indeed that he was actually married to her, and it is said that he carried her portrait about with him. Prior to his trial he persisted in assuring his solicitor that she was the companion with whom he had arranged to travel to Brighton on the day of Gold's murder . . . After last Friday he assured his solicitor that having written to the lady expressing sorrow for his conduct in vilifying her name, he had just received from her a reply granting her forgiveness and enclosing him some flowers. It is almost needless to add that whether on Lefroy's part this be a delusion or a wilful mis-statement, Miss Cameron has never written to the convict or sent him any flowers.

(*The Daily Telegraph* 28/11/1881)

And the following story appeared in several newspapers:

On one occasion it was alleged that a cabman brought Miss Cameron a letter while she was performing at a London theatre, telling her that Mr Henderson, a well-known theatrical manager, had been thrown down in the street and had both his legs broken, and that he had been conveyed to a hotel, where he wished to see her. This appeared to be so bona-fide that Miss Cameron was preparing to go as desired, when fortunately the cabman was asked who sent the letter, and he replied that it had been given him by a gentleman near the theatre who told him to drive the lady to London Bridge Station. In this way the strange plot was baulked. The handwriting of the letter has been identified as Lefroy's.

Despite denying that she knew Lefroy, Violet Cameron was not believed, and she was besieged by reporters at the Comedy Theatre.

20

Monday 28th November.

With 24 hours to go, the morning arrived with still no news from the Home Office. Dutton wrote one last desperate letter to Sir William Harcourt:

Not having received any reply to my letter yesterday and the time fixed for the execution of my unhappy client so rapidly drawing near, will you grant me an interview this afternoon that I may lay before you all the facts that have come to my knowledge in connection with him, upon hearing which I feel confident that you will consider the execution should be stayed until the truth has been ascertained both as regards those facts and the state of mind.

There was still a faint chance that a reprieve might arrive at the last moment as had happened 10 years earlier at the prison when a woman, Christina Edmunds – who was due to be executed for poisoning a little boy – was reprieved and sent to Broadmoor lunatic asylum. But by 5pm Dutton had still not received any reply from the Home Office.

At the prison, the preparations for the execution were almost complete. Workmen were busy fixing a flagstaff over the entrance of the gaol, upon which the black flag was to be hoisted immediately after the sentence was carried out, and a tarpaulin was erected in front of the scaffold to prevent the gaze of curious sightseers from outside the walls.

All day long the occupants of every cab emerging from the local station were closely scanned by people to see if they contained anyone connected with the case. Towards nightfall, a medium-built God-fearing man in his early sixties, dressed in a dark yellowish brown suit and wearing a low hat, was seen slipping into the prison. He looked like a farm bailiff. He had a moustache and whiskers and his hair was slightly grizzled.

Earlier that day he had travelled from Manchester to Brighton and visited his sister, who ran a small shop. He had then booked himself into the Dolphin Hotel. But this was a ruse, for the man's name was William Marwood and he was the public executioner. (That morning he had been at Strangeways Prison in Manchester to 'execute' John Simpson for the murder of his sweetheart, Annie Ratcliffe.) He intended to sleep at the prison that night.

Born in 1820, Marwood was a chatty individual who felt greatly honoured by the sign 'Crown Officer' that hung over his shoeshop in Horncastle, Lincolnshire. The shop was more like a museum of criminal relics with coils of rope hanging from its ceiling. He believed himself far superior to Calcraft, his predecessor, who was reputedly kind to animals but less so to his victims whom he 'hung like dogs'. Marwood liked to tell people that 'Calcraft hanged them, but I execute them'. But he himself had a reputation for being callous. On one occasion he had eaten bread and cheese and drunk beer while sitting next to one of his dead victims who was having a cast made of his face. On another, he was so drunk the evening before an execution that he was still intoxicated the following morning and could barely sign the receipt for his five guinea fee. He had not been very actively employed recently and lamented about the 'good old days' when he had hanged as many as four in one day. This was to be his first one in Lewes.

Earlier that day, Marwood had told reporters that, in his opinion, 'the plea of insanity in Lefroy's case was not a strong one, as the convict seemed to talk in a reasonable manner and wrote so sensibly that it was difficult to think there could be insanity.' Furthermore, he condemned the way 'petitions for reprieve were often organised by people who knew nothing about the case'.

Before going to bed, he went to inspect the new gallows apparatus which he himself had designed. He visited a pit dug in the north-east corner of the exercise yard. It was 15ft deep, was bricked up and could be entered by the 14 steps which led to its bottom. It was covered by a platform consisting of a double trapdoor constructed on a level with the ground. The traps were kept up by a lever worked by the side of the wooden gallows: there were no steps, ladder or elevated stand involved. Lefroy would simply have to step upon the platform and at a signal the lever would drop him in the deep well below.

Meanwhile, the man at the centre of all this activity, spent his final day writing to his friends and family. His last letters, unless the authorities objected, would be posted after his execution. In the afternoon, he was persuaded to take some exercise in the yard, but he seemed so weak that he had to be helped back to his cell. In the evening, according to unofficial reports, he relapsed into the calm, stolid mood which had been so apparent during his trial.

The chaplain visited him and told him that any hopes of a respite were gone. Lefroy was calm, thanked him for his kindness over the last few weeks and asked him if he wanted the flowers his little cousin Melville had brought him for the chapel. Cole said he did. Then Lefroy gave him a bundle of blue-lined sheets of prison writing paper and talked about their content. The chaplain agreed to have a look at them in his office. Then Cole prayed together with the prisoner.

Lefroy spent the rest of the evening scanning the books which had been supplied to him, reading extracts from one and then another until about half-past ten. He then knelt by his bedside for some time apparently praying silently, as he had done every night since his incarceration. Afterwards, he undressed and went to bed.

PART TWO

A ROMANCE
OF REAL LIFE

21

In the late 1990s, to great nervous excitement, I discovered a bundle of papers at the Public Records Office at Kew. The writing was familiar to me, for it had a unique style. The first person pronoun was often joined on to the verb, 'I should' becoming 'Ishould'. I had first seen it on the original wanted posters for Lefroy which had displayed samples of his handwriting. These 48 sheets of blue-lined paper, stamped with the Lewes Prison insignia, were undoubtedly those which Lefroy had given Thomas Cole, the chaplain.

But they did not simply contain a confession which had been alluded to in various articles about the case over the years. Incredibly, the bundle of papers contained a 19,000-word autobiography which Lefroy had written in just 11 days while in prison. It opened in dramatic style:

MY AUTOBIOGRAPHY

Preface

It may be asked by what right and from what motives do I presume to set on paper the story of such a life as mine, and in anticipation of such questions arising I have determined to answer them before they are asked. Firstly, as to my motives which are as follows: that as a great deal of false glamour, mock heroism and falsehood has been thrown over the fearful tragedy of June 27 thereby causing the most awful occurrence to be looked upon in a false light, which may cause untold harm to the unthinking or ignorant in the future, to prevent which if possible I the only living person who holds the key to the mystery, have determined to draw aside the drawn down curtain of the Past and lay the awful tragedy bare before the world in all its terror, wickedness, and black unfathomable despair.

Secondly, that I most earnestly desire to exonerate from participation or knowledge of this crime all those unfortunate persons on whom suspicion or the breath of suspicion has been cast. I need hardly say I refer more particularly to Mr Thomas Gold and even more so to my noble, devoted, misjudged cousin, Mr F.W. Seale.

Thirdly, to remove that possibly natural but most injurious idea that because a young man does not drink, smoke, gamble, bet or indulge in acts of profligacy he is never likely to commit any crime.

And people who have read of my sin and its consequences together with my poverty have no doubt with a shrug of their shoulders observed 'Oh, of course the fellow had been living a "fast life",' little thinking that to every one of the above indictments I could plead 'not guilty' having been practically a teetotaller from my birth, never smoking until last June, and only once in my life having played cards for money three years ago. I have never in my life betted in a race of any sort and no one, whatever may be my faults, has ever accused me of being profligate. And yet in spite of all this I <u>fell</u>.

Fourthly, that in the cause of morality I consider the reasons which led to the committal of this awful crime <u>should have equal publicity with the crime itself</u>.

Lastly, that I pen this sad story, this tragedy of real life in the sincere and earnest hope that it may cause some young man, ambitious, careless and unscrupulous as I once was to pause, reflect and <u>stop</u> in his Hell bound career, before it is <u>too late</u>. Too late for reparation, too late to heal the wounded hearts of those you love. Too late for all, for everything but repentance.

One word more and I have finished. Everything mentioned by me hereafter is an <u>incident of my life</u> as it really happened. I have given the real names of persons in every instance but one, and that one is the person I have called 'May Gordon', which is not her real name. That dear name will go forever undivulged, and I should consider it little short of profanity to introduce it here. I may mention that I have given everyone their real name not to needlessly drag them into publicity but simply to show that I am relating a romance of <u>real life</u> and not one of fiction. I have endeavoured to avoid wounding the feelings of anyone but at the same time I have only felt it my duty to expose falsehood or misconception wherever it has occurred.

My weary, storm beaten career is closing fast. Everyday my life is drawing nearer to its close and my soul to its Maker. Literally am I now 'In the Dark Valley of the Shadow of Death' and that these my dying words of <u>truth and warning</u> may go forth far and wide somewhere to ripen and bring forth good seed, is the last and fervent prayer of

Percy Lefroy Mapleton, Lewes Gaol, November 17 1881

The first two chapters deal with Lefroy's childhood, to which I have alluded earlier. In chapter 3 he writes about a strange experience he had in Australia.

One cold, wet stormy night I was walking down Swanson Street, terribly ill and feeble in body but worse, far worse in mind. For nearly two days not an atom of food had passed my lips. I had slept out the night before and got drenched with rain, and now crawling down the lengthy street I came, staggering along catching at iron railings or any other support as I went, deathly cold and yet burnt up with fever. The shops had been long shut for it was nearly twelve o'clock at night, and consequently but few persons were about.

On, on I went, now walking a few yards and then resting for a minute, ere I proceeded. And where was I going? I was going to do what I had often done before, creep under a small boat which lay bottom upwards on Edward's boat yard by the river Yarra, and to this cold, miserable shelter I was looking as eagerly forward to, as if I had been going to rest my aching limbs upon the softest bed that ever a mortal laid upon. But even this was denied me, for on reaching the place I found that my boat had been locked up with the rest! It may seem childish, but on learning this I sat down on the wharf and cried like a child. I was so utterly broken down in spirit that this last calamity - for calamity it was to me - seemed more than I could bear.

I had no strength to move from where I was, though it was raining fast and already I was chilled to the bone, but sat there, gazing at the gloomy river at my feet. And as I sat there looking at it a spirit of Satan entered in my heart whispering first, but getting bolder by degrees, that here in the rushing water at my feet was rest: horrified at the bare idea I rose to my feet and turned to leave the dangerous spot, but then the thought arose where was I to go? Pass yet another night upon those dreadful stones, that mocked me to my face, every time they rang out sharply beneath my weary head? Pass yet another night under the distant stars that shed their light upon me with such cruel coldness, seeming to hold themselves aloof from all the world below, and showing all such abject ones as I our lowliness and sin by virtue of their height? No, no, that could not be.

Again I wandered back and looked down with now a different feeling at my heart and with an oar lying there, tried hard to find the river's depth. Down, down deeper and deeper went the oar and now my hand itself was in the water and I found no depth. Nine good deep feet of rushing water, black as ink and cold as ice and yet they promised rest. Only a little leap, whispered the tempter, a brief struggle and then you are at rest: no more hunger, cold or fatigue but everlasting rest, only a little leap is wanted. My mind was made up. Yes, yes, it was all true, and never giving a thought to the life beyond the grave where suicides are punished, I resolved to plunge into the stream. There was no fear of interruption. No one came this way, and the bridge was too far off in the inky darkness for anyone to see me, though I myself, could see the gas lights on it flickering in the wind. And then getting on the extreme brink I stood upright and took one last sad farewell look upon the world I was so soon to leave.

It was a splendid night for such a deed as this! I remember the pretty bridge throwing its shadows down upon the stream, and making even that look blacker than before. From where I was I could see reflected in the water the yellow of the gas lights and somehow, then, in my half frenzied state, they seemed like eyes that looked at me from far beyond the grave, inviting me to come and share their rest. How the wind howled and shrieked among the gloomy gum trees on the river's bank? Once, even twice, I could have sworn my name was called and turned half guilty and afraid, to find it but the wind. A treacherous, noisy wind it was that drove thick waves of clouds before it as if to give the stars a curtain that they too might not see the deed of sin below. No thought of those at home once crossed my mind. Nothing but a vague awful longing for rest and black utter despair.

I took one last look at the distant lights of the city, held up my hands above my head, so that I might jump out well into the stream; shut my eyes and was bending my body for the leap, when the thought suddenly flashed upon me that I had letters about me which would cause my body when found to be immediately identified. This must not be. I had no hesitation in condemning my family to years and years of the most awful suspense, but I could not bear that they should know I had committed suicide. So retreating a few paces, I put my hand in the inside pocket of my coat, pulled out my wallet, and proceeded to tear into fragments every atom of paper it contained, throwing them as I did so into the gloomy stream below. They were quickly borne away by the rapid current and as I watched them fade into the murky darkness, I envied their good fortune and wished that I was there as well. Then I felt my finger touch a piece of paper in a little pocket in which something was wrapped up. Wondering what it could be, I opened it and something small and soft lay in my hand, I was about to throw it away and take the fateful leap, when an extraordinary feeling surely sent by God, impelled me, tired, weary and ill as I was, to crawl up to the bridge and there by the lamp light look at what I had found.

Yes, there it lay, a tiny golden lock, cut from my darling's hair! Unremembered, unheard in my madness, it yet was surely sent by God to save my soul from death.

As I stood looking at it, feeling as one might feel who slowly awaking from a trance, the great clock in the city peeled out the hour 1 am. And as the sound reached my ears what a great flood of memories came rushing to my brain. I thought of another chime, that had rung out in dear old Ventnor when I had won the great first love of a pure and loving heart. I thought of the dear faces so far away, and then there came into my ear a loving voice that said 'God bless you and goodbye'.

And then as if I had been gradually led up to see it, the awful enormity of the crime I had been about to commit flashed like lightning upon me, and there with my head pillowed upon the cold stone I humbly asked for pardon.

It is significant that it is during this portion of his story – a period of great loneliness – that Lefroy for the first time introduces 'May Gordon' to the reader. But the references are mysterious: first meeting her at Ventnor; a lock of hair falling onto the ground; a voice stopping him from doing something awful (so similar to his experience in the 'Ventnor' letter of 1878).

On his return to England (in chapter 4) , Lefroy goes to stay with his cousin Anne Clayton and her family at Wallington:

My life at Wallington was very happy for the next few months. I knew no one there but my own relatives, but I was quite content. I was deeply attached to my cousin's two dear little children, and led even a quiet life. Surely the calm before the awful storm.

He soon learns about the success of 'May Gordon' and is about to embark, in his words, on a 'bitter fight for bread and fame'. He goes and watches May perform. 'Refreshed by a sight of her sweet young face,' he decides not to contact her until he has found fame and fortune:

She should never know of my return until I could present myself worthily before her. No thought of the lingering suspense I was dooming her to entered my mind, for I believed I was doing what was right . . . I told my dear cousin [Anne Clayton] a little of the one touch of romance in my life, though of course not all. In her I found, as I have ever found, the sympathy of a dear and loving sister. Whatever desires of an ambitious nature I had were never for myself but simply that I might make a name and position worthy to offer May. Her sweet young face was ever in my thoughts, and I had less compunction in not communicating with her, as I knew from several reliable sources that though admired by many she was engaged to none, and had already refused two or three most excellent offers of marriage. . . But I was still as ambitious and uneasy as ever, for every day May's popularity seemed increasing, which only made me more desperate. If only I had had the sense to write to her and explain my position I might not have been in this awful position now.

In 1880 Lefroy manages to obtain the commission to write the Christmas pantomime for the Croydon Theatre, and he writes that he was 'getting on famously' when his aunt, 'whom I nearly idolized,' died after a painful illness:

She had been long troubled with a racking cough that seemed to shake her terribly (for she was nearly seventy years of age) but nevertheless she was always gentle and loving to me and ready to take an interest in anything I did. I shall never forget her death. All day long, that fourth of November, she had been lying, gasping for breath, and every now and again in excruciating pain, but towards mid-night, a change began to take place and here I may ask what can be more solemn than a death bed? I know of nothing. Somehow it seems to me that one sees or rather feels the greatness of the Almighty more than at any other period of life. I was sitting, facing the bed on which she lay, while on one side was her daughter, on the other her son. No one had spoken for some time, but at last my dear aunt opening her eyes and looking fondly at me, whilst she clasped her son's hand in hers, said 'Promise me that you'll always watch over him'. Poor Frank silently pressed her hand and almost heartbroken turned his head away, too overcome to speak. As for me I was in a like condition. All her loving words and deeds, years and years of the purest motherly love, came before my eyes as if I were looking at some panoramic view of all the past. Oh, how I mourned for all the careless and ungrateful words I had spoken to her and then would have given anything to live my young life once over again with her and treat her differently. But vain regrets have never yet stayed for an instant Death's far reaching hand when once the fiat has gone forth. And so it was now. As the dim light fell upon the dying face before me I saw the eyes open and give one last loving look, and they closed for ever on this mortal earth. In an instant I had touched the jet of gas and a flood of light streamed down upon the placid face, but there was suspense. Upon those lips, never more to give me words of loving welcome, there lay a sweet and happy smile, as if she who wore it was only asleep and dreaming of some quiet and glorious reality. And then we sat, grief stricken and alone, whispering comfort to each other. Whilst, had I but known what was before me, I would have implored the saviour of the world then and there to lay me struck by death's icy hand in rest and innocence beside the one already taken from us.

22

Lefroy entitles his chapter 5 'The Trail of the Serpent'. In it he tells of his first meeting with Henry Bracy and his deception over the 'Offenbach' opera.

I called upon Mr Bracy at the Globe and directly I saw his happy, genial face, my heart reproached me bitterly for the deception I was practising. To cut a long story short before we had been talking half an hour I conceived a great liking for the handsome kindly young actor. He was well-known in Melbourne having often acted there, so I had to be very cautious in playing the difficult role of a native Australian, but thanks to my excellent memory and early training in deceit, I got through my task though not without several times wishing I could muster up courage to confess the truth and earnestly ask him for his friendship and forgiveness. However, by the time I left, there was no retreat open and the deadly game once commenced I had to carry it through even to the bitter end. Mr Bracy, I must say all this while, believed me to be by documentary and verbal evidence the secretary of Mr Coppin, and a young colonial journalist of some little position. Every day the plot thickened. Bracy and I often saw each other, not infrequently lunching together, and I can honestly say I never endeavoured to obtain money from him at these or any other times.

So far, this scheme had succeeded. I was daily getting to know more and more literary men and actors of repute, and consequently hoped very soon to obtain some substantial benefit from this knowledge. I had asked Mr Bracy, as stage manager of the Globe, to try and get a little commedietta of mine played, and with, I believe the most genuine kindness he promised his utmost to do so. Of course this false life was very expensive to me, for 'sponging' (if I may be pardoned for using this slangy but expressive word to you) was never one of my faults, and consequently I was living very much more extravagantly than I ought to have done. But the thought that I was getting nearer to May, buoyed me up, and I was never happier than when hearing her praised or adored. For all I knew, she believed me still in Australia, and though I had often several narrow escapes of being 'introduced' to her, I always escaped in time, and we had never seen each other since that gloomy winter's morning nearly four years before. But a terrible change was at hand.

One very hot evening in May I was sitting with a friend (whom I shall call Fielding) in the newly decorated smoking room of the Junior Garrick Club, of which club he was a member, talking on various subjects theatric, when he said rather abruptly, concerning a particular play, 'I don't think much of her. Give me Lord ——'s fiancé for that'. 'Who is she?' I asked, cautiously looking at the blue rings of smoke that went curling up to the ceiling. 'Why May Gordon of course. I thought every one knew that.'

That night I walked aimlessly up and down the embankment for hours letting the soft night air play upon my heated brow and wishing that it might cool also the flames of maddening jealousy and despair that were raging in my heart and soul.

Lefroy entitles his chapter 6 'The Lights of London' after a George Sims play that was being performed in the West End at the time he was in prison.

To say that for the next day or two I was utterly demented, would be I am sure no mere figure of speech. I could do nothing, think of nothing but May. For two whole days I stayed at home never going out except at night and then only to wander up and down some gloomy road where I could think of all that I had lost and loved. Fielding's words I found (as I thought) to be quite true for had I not seen her twice talking mainly to a well dressed rather effeminate looking young man, who was walking with herself and mother, and whom I learned was a frequent visitor at their pretty little suburban villa. What did it matter to me that this 'lordship' was known to them as plain 'Mr Harrison', it only made the matter worse in my eyes, for before any breath of scandal should touch my darling through his conduct, I would shoot him down and give my own life to save her fair name. Now that my eyes were opened I saw how cruelly neglectful I had been to my darling in never once letting her know that I was dead or alive. All the three years she had been faithful to me, and now was it to be wondered at that she could seek for honest love elsewhere. If I could not beat my adversary with his own weapon, falsehood, I would give in broken-hearted and despairing though I might be, to his marrying her in his own name. But let him once approach her with any other offer and his life should pay the penalty. What happened to me I could not care if my life could save her honour I should be well content. So in my delirium I went to Vaughan's the gunsmith's in the Strand and purchased a six chambered revolver, bought cartridges elsewhere, loaded it, and went about my daily associations with the deadly weapon ever ready at my hand. It was no mere jealousy of my rival that prompted this. If he married her, and legitimately beat me in the unequal contest of rank and wealth versus poverty and obscurity, well and good, I should have accepted my fate though life would have seemed to have lost all charm for me, but if he adopted another course, then let his blood be upon his own head. Those were my thoughts and may God in his infinite mercy forgive my entertaining them for an instant.

Having a pretty fertile imagination I was not long in hitting upon the only way in which I could possibly meet Lord — at all. His rank of course I could not emulate, though as that was unknown to May, I was not so concerned about it, but his wealth I could counterfeit possibly. I had hit upon no definite scheme when one day I accidentally heard that Bracy was a sort of relative of Miss Gordon and possessed very great influence with both May and her mother.

This decided me at once. That evening I wrote a letter to Mr Bracy apologising for not having done so before, and telling him I had received a great shock in just learning by telegram that my old friend and employer, Mr Coppin (who was travelling to England with the score of the opera via San Francisco) had just died of apoplexy leaving me the opera and £1,000 a year which was to be increased to £10,000 per annum <u>when I married</u>. After going on to express (my really genuine) liking for him, I concluded by <u>asking him to accept the opera as a slight tribute of friendship and regard</u>. My object being to make our interests identical, and to get him through feelings of gratitude to aid me in my fight against my rival. Of course he to present me in the name of Lefroy and in the position of a wealthy man to let May believe I had changed my name by Mr Coppin's wish, and then to do my utmost to win back her love once more. A very insane reckless scheme on paper, and yet really (not) quite so mad as it seemed. I should not have to place the opera, or rather an opera, in Bracy's hands before two months had expired. And my assumed role, except for the want of the main thing, money, was not a difficult one. I was well educated, had a fair superficial knowledge of most subjects, was well dressed, accustomed to good society and by birth a gentleman, not by any means the combination of card sharper, shopsman and pickpocket that has occasionally been represented.

But the great stumbling block was how to <u>keep up</u> the character of a wealthy man? For the next month or so I might excuse myself from doing this, but yet not longer for suspicion once aroused I knew I should be lost. But with a certain hope like Mr Micawber that something would 'turn up' I rushed in desperation headlong to my doom. All this time my dear friends were naturally anxious as to what made me go to town nearly every day, and remain so late at night. So agreed I to add another lie to the already fearfully long list and say I was engaged on the staff of the 'Era' at four guineas a week paid monthly which would not fall due <u>until the last Saturday in June</u>. This I induced them to believe and so put it out of their reach to help me at all. Thus I was leading or beginning to lead a double life, impersonating not only two characters but both at the same time.

In May I severed my connection with the 'Herald', the proprietor naturally being annoyed at the careless way in which I worked for him. So at the end of May I should have been entirely without means had not my article on Melbourne been accepted by a London magazine, the *Argosy*, for which I received £8 10s. All this time Bracy and I were becoming daily more intimate. I can truly say I was deeply attached to him and should he ever read this I trust he will believe that even I was not <u>all bad</u>. We often dined together sometimes at his club, the United Arts, or at his house where I met his wife and was treated by her with the greatest kindness. Bracy's gratitude for my generous kindness, as he called it, used to cut me to the heart, and had it not been for my hopeless love for May I should have thrown off the acted lie with horror and disgust. But my astonishment may be imagined when one day I found that my 'rival' was but a nightmare, no designing peer, but an old friend of Mrs Gordon's but was very unpopular with May. And so I had to keep up the pretence without having to fight any opponent at all. And now my affairs were truly becoming desperate. Very often of an evening I would drop in to the Strand Theatre for half an hour's chat with Bracy or Messrs Marcus, Ashley or Cox, whoever might be off the stage for the time. These gentlemen were all very kind, genial men, particularly M. Marcus and I got to liking him only second to Bracy.

One hot evening at the beginning of June while sitting there talking I challenged the Strand Theatre Cricket Club to play a match at their ground at St John's Wood against eleven colonial journalists selected by me. This was at once accepted by letter and I think June 17 was the day fixed for the match. It must not be thought that this was departing from my scheme, on the contrary I relied upon it to strengthen the already good feeling existing between Bracy and myself, for the instant I placed the forged opera (by a well known English comic opera composer person) in his hands I intended to ask him to introduce me to May. On the 24th instant I was promised a loan of £100 (to be paid in monthly instalments of £5) by a person in whom I had the greatest confidence, so I had no fear for myself after the end of the month. But how to get over my present necessities was the thing, so I determined with a good deal of reluctance and horror at my deceit to ask for a loan of six pounds from my earliest Wallington friend – Mr W.H. Gutteridge. He lent it me willingly, believing me to be in a good appointment and on the understanding that I should pay at least half of it <u>by the end of June</u>.

The day for the cricket match came and went. We had a most enjoyable day, no one there would have imagined the awful heart-sickness I was suffering from. My eleven consisted of various personal friends of my own including Messrs. Loridan and Parry, then of the Strand Theatre, who filled up two vacancies in the eleven, while our opponents were Messrs. Morris, R.Reece, Bracy, Ashley, Hiller etc. etc., several well known gentlemen. We won the match and then to my horror I found that my bag had been cut open and money taken from it, and to get home I had to borrow a few shillings from Bracy. I need hardly say the things pawned by me represent the various stages of desperation I passed into. And so the month went on. I raised money right and left and had it not been for the hundred pounds I was to receive at the end of the month I should have been utterly lost. I need hardly say that such a life as I was living was most terribly trying, and I felt utterly broken down as the mental strain was so great.

At last the prayed for 24th of June arrived and my liabilities were as follows. I owed about 30 shillings to Bracy, three pounds to Mr Gutteridge, a pound or so to my cousins and I had all my clothes to redeem. Bracy believed I was entering on possession of my thousand a year on the following Monday, June 27. In a day or two I had to put without fail (if I wished to keep up my false position) the opera in Bracy's hands and I could not do this unless I handed over to the composer £50 before the 28th June. While as if this was not enough I needed my subscription of three guineas to the United Arts Club of which I had been elected a member. It will thus be seen that in the event of my failing to satisfy nearly all these persons, utter ruin must have followed. The falsehood of my life would have been seen through and May and I would have been parted without doubt for ever. And so I say the most momentous day of my life dawned and in high spirits I went up to Charing Cross Station to meet my friend (Lester I will call him), in the First Class waiting room there. When I entered he was sitting near the door, a couple of portmanteaux at his side labelled 'Paris', where I remembered he had told me he was going en route for Madrid. I may say here that I had lent him when I came into my 35 pounds, ten guineas, and he had promised to pay it several times, at last when my patience was almost wearied he wrote to me saying he should come into a couple of thousand pounds at the end of June and if I could wait a few weeks longer, he would pay me on the 24th – what he owed and would moreover lend me any sum up to a hundred I might require. As I entered, Lester rose hastily, 'There you are boy, rather late, but never mind. Here's your cheque. I know you'll pay it off as quick as you can. Wish you luck. Goodbye, take care of yourself' and so saying he shook my hand warmly and pressed into it a piece of paper and was gone. He had been so quick that I had scarcely time to thank him, but the feeling of entire relief at my heart drove all other feelings away as walking hastily down the Strand I turned into Child's Bank with the cheque and had it instantly returned marked 'no effects'.

What followed I can never remember with distinctiveness. I remember going and sitting for hours in St James' Park watching the morning turn into evening, and the evening into night. I remember getting up and staggering through the noisy streets about 11 o'clock to catch the last tram for Wallington. People spoke to me at home, but I don't remember what they said. I went to bed and all that lovely Sunday I went about like a man in a dream, thinking of nothing but my utter ruin. In the evening I walked down with Seale at his own request to his mother's grave and there with the shadows falling round us we shed bitter tears for her we had loved so well. But by the time we reached home my heart was filled again with blackness and despair. I sat up in the darkened parlour looking out upon the glorious summer night while slowly and surely the tempter of all took possession of my heart. Whispering, whispering to me that I must get at least ten pounds by tomorrow night and that the only way of getting it was by force. Murder was only dreadful in name, when it was done I should feel just as usual, for had not my favourite writer George R. Sims said in *The Referee* that murderers walked and talked and felt just as any other man might do, and that the hand of Cain and all that was nonsense. Besides there need not be any murder only a shot to disable and then robbery was easy, especially in a railway carriage argued the tempter. Say in an express train going to Brighton, surely plenty of wealthy people would be in it; there could be no failure, no deadly struggle would result. One shot and all would be done. A mere movement of the finger, and I had the means of staving off discovery. Of course went on the evil one it would perhaps take the matter into the regions of moral certainty if you took some other weapon with you, <u>say a razor</u>. Muster up courage and May Gordon shall yet be yours. Give in, and I leave you to your fate, exposed, ruined and disgraced. The law will be put in motion against you and the girl you love shall recoil from you with horror. Even now I can hear the hellish words ringing in upon my ear, as terror struck I recoiled in horror from my own black thoughts, but alas! It was the old story of Faust and Mephistopheles over again. And I sold my soul for the promise of a woman's love.

As the miserable compact was signed and sealed, a strange sad voice called twice my name. I rushed to the window but there was no one there, nothing to be seen but the evening sky reddened in the distance by the lights of London, which fell upon the sombre clouds like the reflection of a mighty fire.

23

The morning of the last day of my holding out dawned. Just before my cousin Mr Clayton left he came into my room where I was in bed and asked me when I was going to give him up those things belonging to him which I had pledged. Wearily turning my face to the wall I said 'tonight, without fail' and he left me. I had already promised Seale to pay him what I owed him this same evening. Soon after nine I got up, went downstairs and in pursuance of my plan conceived the night before I wrote the note purporting it came from Mrs Clayton, and sent it to Mr Ellis. My dear little cousins careered into the room, but I did not play with them as was my wont, for I hardly saw them, my very heart seemed gone and in its place a raging spirit lay concealed and moved me as he pleased.

My cousin's little pupils entered, and one of them said 'You do look strange. Don't you feel well?' 'Well,' and then I rushed upstairs with yet (another) echo ringing in my heart. At last Mr Ellis came, I rushed swiftly from the house, into his shop, obtained the money, said goodbye to my cousin, feeling as if I should never see her again, and then walked as fast as I could to Waddon Station, where I caught the 10.50 from Wallington. London Bridge was soon reached. Out of the carriage, down the steps, straight along the street and then into the gloomy door over which hung three golden balls. No delay anywhere, all ready, everything favourable for no more willing servant is there, than the Devil, when by it he gains a complete mastery afterwards. It did not take long to redeem the revolver, and there I had it once more in my hands. One shot and all would be over, so argued the spirit of darkness and you will be free once more from this awful poverty. But I had something more to do yet. I had not sufficient for my fare to Brighton, so going to the office of a friend, not Seale let it be most distinctly understood, I borrowed five shillings and with that and the money already in my possession I had funds to lunch at the International Restaurant in the Approach and later London Bridge Station.

And now that I have bared thus far the most awful secret of my heart I will repeat step by step the awful tragedy, what I did, what

I felt, and what I thought, shall all be exposed for the first time to the world. Supposition and uncertainty shall cease and all I ask [is] that these poor words of a dying and <u>most earnestly repentant man</u>, may be implicitly believed, however I may ask my readers to discount the evidence of certain witnesses. Let it be remembered moreover that I am the only living person that can clear up the mystery and intend doing so in every way. And to depict the occurrences of this awful day more vivid I shall avail myself of a literary license and do so in the first person. The first thing was to get my ticket: tending 12/6 to the clerk (not a sovereign for I had none about me) I got my ticket and left the window there being no ladies anywhere near at any time I was there. [At the trial it was alleged that he had paid with a sovereign and that there were women in the queue behind him.] Going into the waiting room, my next proceeding was to load the revolver which I did under cover of a newspaper. This done, after cocking it and feeling that the razor was secure in my pocket I made my way onto the platform. It was now just three minutes to two. Walking past the First Class carriage I looked in, and saw to my great satisfaction that one compartment was occupied by only a single passenger. After entering and as I put my head out of the window to shut the door, I saw an old gentleman getting into a carriage some way down the train.

Sitting down, with my face to the engine on the near side, I drew out my paper and under cover of it proceeded to carefully scrutinise my companion. He had a paper bag of fruit with him. Strawberries I thought and he apparently did not like me to see him eating them for he put them in the rack above as I entered. Somehow the tempter did not seem to have got such a hold on me when the train started for I shuddered immediately at the base idea of shooting the unconscious man opposite. Very well, said the Devil, how are you going to get back from Brighton if you don't get money on the road? I looked at him again. He was a short slight man about forty with dark hair and whiskers. And every now and then he would look at me in a very peculiar way. Could he have known what I've come for? He had a gold watch I could see that and rings, but I did not like his looks. It seemed as if he knew I came to murder him. I looked out of the window. We were coming to a station, East Croydon. Now should I try or not: I wandered if – but all the time he was looking steadily at me again and his eyes seemed to pierce into my soul.

I could stand it no longer and got out of the compartment, my companion little thinking that to his inquisitive looks he probably owed his life. As I was walking down all the carriages, looking in at the windows to see if any First Class passenger was by himself, there came into my heart once more those loving words 'God bless you and goodbye'. But this time they found no response. The person hearing them was not in soul the one to whom they were first spoken. No, no, this man with murder in his mind was someone else in my poor earthly form, and so the mocking laugh that came unheeded to my lips, consigned those loving words to the black and bitter holes in my heart to be drowned, spurned and lost by all the evil spirits raging there. At this moment in passing a First Class compartment I saw it was tenanted by only one person, whether young or old I could not tell, for his head was completely covered with a handkerchief, which as I entered he removed, and I saw before me for the first time in my life Mr Gold. He was there sitting nearly in the middle seat with his back to the engine. I nearly in front of him, facing the engine in the rear corner.

When the train started Mr Gold was looking out of the window and I was ostensibly reading the paper. On, on through the dear familiar scenery rushed the train, reminding me, had I been really there, of many and many a cherished walk with those I loved. But of none of these things was I thinking now, as I sat there with fixed and staring eyes, my hand slowly drawing the deadly weapon from its hiding place. Every minute of waiting seemed an hour, we were rushing now through streets fast and I knew that soon the yawning gulf of blackness would be upon us. The pistol was now in my right hand, loaded, cocked and <u>levelled</u>. Oh God! How can I write what follows! Quicker and quicker flew the train, higher and higher rose the chalky walls on either side, and fiercer and fiercer raged a battle in my heart not yet long commenced, but which, in these few seconds was to decide my earthly fate for ever. Which was it to be, a pistol shot, money and happiness? Or innocence and all my false and hollow life laid bare?

Quick, no time for reflection. Higher and higher rose the walls of chalk, shutting out all sight of heaven and telling me that now I must decide for once, for ever. Nearer and nearer, closer and closer, the yawning mouth was close upon us. Fifty yards, thirty, ten, five we were in! Slowly I closed my eyes, extended my arm and fired, and eased the trigger back. The engine gave an awful shriek, like the last bitter cry of my good spirit, as it flew in terror from me and I was in darkness, both of soul and body. As the report died away I sprang to my feet and peered into the gloom where my unoffending victim had been sitting. Had I killed him? No, no, for in an instant he was upon me, not before though, in my madness I had discharged three or four more shots at him. Oh merciful Father give me strength to finish now. In an instant I was extended on the ground up against the furthest door, keeping at bay as well as I could the justly infuriated man, who with one hand grasped me by the throat and with the other, struck me savagely upon the head with the revolver, which he grasped by the handle, striking me with the end of the muzzle. Not a word was uttered and there in the darkness of the tunnel that death struggle commenced. The awful blackness of the tunnel without, the air laden with the fearful smell of powder, the half gloom of that living grave, only made visible by the feeble light above which shed its sickly light upon the livid face that fiercely looked in mine, made such a fearful impression on me that never, if I lived a thousand years, could I forget it. Poor Mr Gold who might have been unwounded for any effect it had upon him then could easily have pulled the communicator a dozen times, had he wished to do so, but he never appeared to think of it. As for me I was a mere child in his hands and I had as much as I could do to save myself from being throttled when he threw the pistol on one side and tried to grasp my throat with both his hands.

And so the time sped on, and our positions never changed, he pincering me to the ground whilst I as strenuously resisted neither being armed and both being on the floor of the carriage at the same end as the door he entered at London Bridge. Never once was there any 'scuffling or fighting standing up', from the time the first shot was fired until within a few miles of Balcombe. Mrs Brown and her daughter must be either genuinely mistaken as to the train, or telling a wilful falsehood. At last the venue of the deadly struggle changed. All at once, as if by mutual agreement we released each other. Both maddened with fury and <u>both</u> believing they were fighting for their lives. I had still the same utter soullessness, if I may use the expression, but this was also increased by a fresh feeling, that of mad desperation. I <u>knew</u> that if we <u>both</u> arrived at Brighton, my fate was sealed, and I did not know but that we might be quite close there, for every minute that had passed had seemed at least to me, as if were laden with the weight of years. And now before Mr Gold could prevent me I had sprung up and throwing open the door, called to him in a voice as of some demon fresh from Hell below, that made me start and tremble when I heard it, to jump from the train or I'd shoot him, at the same time snatching up the pistol. And then with the train flying along at fifty miles an hour, the door wide open and the floor already slipping with blood, the awful ending came. A mad refusal, my hands a pull at a brittle chain, heaving backwards and forwards, turning and twisting, blade against pistol, another shriek from the engine, black, bitter darkness, a sudden jerk, an awful cry, a door quickly shut and I found myself alone.

Alone, my God, alone. When every foot of space was peopled with diverse bloody faces that glared at me whichever way I looked. When every stroke the engine piston made shrieked murder, a cry re-echoed and re-echoed back and back again by thirty thousand feverish voices in my ears. When bleeding hands were on my throat, not once or twice but thirty times a minute. Hands that when I beat them off returned more savagely to the charge than ever. When every sound was lulled by wild despairing cries that seemed to come from out the yawning abyss at my feet, cries that were taken up by grinning imps with fiendish voices as some wild night chorus to their song of murder. Was I alone when pistol shots were crashing in my ears and going like a death knell to my heart? Was I alone or was I not in some great endless gulf that led to Hell, where all was gloomy blackness and these ghastly spectres but the messengers of Satan sent to lead me on? Was I alone I ask when every shadow on the wall, and puff of ghastly steam cried 'murderer' and did its very best to hunt me down. Was this I ask all this alone? When everything I touched gave forth hot blood that layed in stagnant pools beneath my feet; or fell unceasingly upon my face like rain and would not be removed. When every breath of foul mephilia air was filled with blood, and left it in the shape of gory spray upon my face. When ever more the blackness had a crimson tinge from out which cries and arose a pair of hands came forth and tried to pull me down to that great gory thing below. Should I no more see daylight but as my doom be forced to stand here till the last great day, going with burning eyes into the devil haunted gloom beyond. Why even now the carriage door was full of them, all trying to get in and pull me out, and all had ghastly faces stained with blood that rushed and poured from hideous gaping wounds, and as it flowed it seemed to be alive with many thousands of tiny hands that clenched and struck and clawed at me as if to pull me down and down to them. When even now the walls, roof, the seats were running blood. No gentle murmurs but a mighty roar of gases that as it fell and rose again like some great crimson tide, saying naught but murder! From side to side I looked but no escape, for everywhere, before, behind or in front were bleeding hands that tried to seize me and to pull me down, while the Dark Deed was acted there before my very eyes a score of times a second, and every time the Body fell into the dark abyss, they shrieked and howled into my ear that I was theirs for ever. Look, how the crimson tide in which I stood was mounting! Higher and higher it came, and there I stood at the window as if spell bound. Hark, how it swayed against my legs and crept and crept much nearer to my face. Was there no escape? Was I to wait and be submerged in that ensanguined stream that now had got so close that there reflected in its awful face I saw the hideous ghastly thing below.

My God, reflected did I say? With frenzied eyes and heart that seemed of stone, I saw it was no reflection but the thing itself, that now was floating up from where it lay, with staring eyes and blood-stained blackened face to hold me in a mad embrace and claim me for its own. Nearer and nearer it comes. I could move but simply went on staring at the dreadful [indistinct word] that was now close up to my breast. And I could feel it now dashing in hot waves around my throat and those great awful arms were opening for that last embrace. Nearer, nearer, and nearer they came, they were after me and pulling my face down to the awful one beneath when there was a loud shriek from the engine, a sudden burst of glorious light and I fell unconscious to the ground.

Chapter 12: From Balcombe to Wallington

[Here Lefroy made a mistake: it should be chapter 8]

I could not have been insensible more than a minute or two I think, but my feelings when I recovered were utterly impossible to describe. I seemed to have been awakened from some most awful dream but the terrible aspect of the carriage soon showed the fearful reality. The most awful horror and remorse seized my soul and I firmly believe that from the previous Sunday night until this moment I had been as insane for the time as any homicidal maniac in Broadmoor. I am not in any way desirous of hiding my guilt but I knew then and I know now that my supposition was correct. I felt, at this moment as a person of gentle disposition and naturally kind-hearted might do if he returned home and was informed that a most atrocious and cold blooded murder had been committed by someone exactly resembling him. Of course now my first thought was self-preservation, and to improve my chances of safety I knew I must dispose of the various articles left by Mr Gold in the carriage. The first thing I hurled out was the revolver which fell in some underwood close to a bridge not very far from the tunnel, on the same side as that on which the other articles were found, but strange to say the razor and a stray cartridge I put into my side overcoat pocket. On the floor was Mr Gold's watch with a small piece of chain attached to it, while on the seat where he had been sitting was the handkerchief he had pulled out of the pocket soon after starting I suppose.

What should I do with the watch, put it in my pocket? No, I might be searched, so hastily I slipped it in my shoe and proceeded to open the purse which I found to contain barely half a sovereign. This then was my gold mine, the harvest that was reward for my guilty act, an old fashioned watch and ten shillings! As I put the empty purse in my pocket there slowly came into my mind those awful words 'What shall it profit a man if he gain the <u>whole world</u> and lose his own soul'. I looked in the glass, and my heart sank as I saw my appearance, ghastly face and covered in blood, (for I may say that in spite of insinuations to the contrary nearly all the blood upon my head, neck and coat came from my own wounds). In this state how could I help being suspected and detained. I could hide the bloody coat by taking it off and throwing it over my arm which I did, but this of course did not hide the state of my trousers or face. Somehow it seemed to me that my bloodstained collar would attract more attention than anything else, so hastily I tore it off and cast it from the window. I was just congratulating myself that I had got rid of everything when to my horror I saw lying in the rack poor Mr Gold's umbrella. I was about to hurl it from the window when I felt the train perceptibly slacking speed. Terrified lest this should be Brighton, I thrust my head from the window and saw that we were rapidly drawing up at a station platform, and when the train came to a dead standstill (which it did for at least a quarter of a minute), I knew from a board nearly opposite, that the station was Hassocks Gate. Now was the time to alight, but before I could carry out my purpose the train was rapidly quickening speed and soon was flying along as fast as ever. With a groan of despair I sunk back in the seat, resolved if at all suspected to make a clean breast of the whole thing. A minute after we entered Clayton Tunnel this momentary good purpose had fled, and I resolved to fight for my life even to the bitter end and in the coming ordeal at the station to use all the Devil's weapons I possessed, to blind them as to what I really was.

On the arrival of the train at Preston Park I saw at once that all tickets would be collected there, so knew that now the struggle must commence. Before the man who opened the door had time to comment on the state of the carriage I asked him 'if I could see a doctor anywhere' and followed this up by telling Gibson, who came up then that time that I had been murderously attacked and by him I was referred to the station master. I could see that all three had some suspicion of something being wrong, and so when the station master suggested I should go to Brighton I at once assented. I was greatly alarmed however by Watson the guard picking the watch by the chain from my shoe and asking me how it got there, to which I replied 'that I knew nothing about it'. The guard then placed it on the seat by my side, and left me. I do not think either Mr Hall or Gibson saw the watch until it was taken out, and <u>I know</u> that they never spoke a word to me on the subject at all. Watson being the only one who did so.

Collector Gibson was sent with me to Brighton. He sitting exactly opposite to me, in the near corner with his back to the engine. He asked me for my name and address. I of course as a matter of policy giving it correctly. I was greatly concerned to get rid of the bit of chain, so on the way I called his attention to the beautiful scenery out of the furthest window, and threw the chain out of the other without in any way attracting his attention. To do this however was not by any means so easy as Lord Coleridge suggested. I am quite ready to believe that poor Mrs Gold made a mistake, but the chain was <u>not</u> attached to the watch by a swivel but instead the watch ring and a link of the chain were united together in an extraordinary way, so that not knowing the spring I had to tear them asunder by means of force.

We arrived at Brighton and went by Gibson's advice <u>straight</u> to the Superintendent's office. I, to escape observation walking as quickly as possible about a couple of feet in advance of Gibson. <u>No one spoke a word to me prior to my reaching the office</u> and then only the clerk. No one touched me in any way or came within several feet. There was a gentleman sitting waiting in the office, but he left almost directly I entered. What Mr Weston swore at my trial on God's Holy word to be the truth, the whole truth and nothing but the truth, was a series of cold, deliberate and cruel lies, and I only hope God will forgive him as readily as a poor sinning mortal like myself does. I do not believe he intended to do me harm. He solely wanted a little cheap notoriety at the expense of committing perjury.

I believe I succeeded in satisfying Mr Hooper's suspicions, and in company with Watson and Gibson went to the Town Hall. I expressed my satisfaction at being able to communicate with the police, but I kept on asking for, and really needed, a doctor, for I felt terribly weak and faint from loss of blood. While I was at the Town Hall waiting for a surgeon, I, happening to put my hand in my overcoat pocket, found to my intense horror, I had still in my possession the razor and Mr Gold's purse. I may say here once and for all, that the only things I had at anytime in my possession belonging to the deceased, were the watch, bit of chain and purse with a few shillings. The purse found on the line <u>was not his</u>, and I take this opportunity of assuring Mrs Gold on the word of a dying man, that my hands never once entered her husband's pockets, and anything else that may be missing must either have been appropriated by those who found the body or else must have been lost in London. He dropped no skull cap and certainly no 'second pocket book'.

But to return. On finding this damning evidence in my pocket I at once requested to be shown the lavatory, Martin and an old man accompanying me. Martin, according to his evidence, must have slept all the while, for instead of going near where he says I did, I proceeded to a closet and stayed there for nearly five minutes, during which time I was actively engaged in ramming the razor and purse down the pipe, where for all I know they may still remain. Coming out I found Martin outside staring at the door. No doctor coming we proceeded to the hospital, Martin and Gibson going with me, though for what reason I am convinced none of them knew. Neither of them are what I should term intellectual men, though Martin had a very dull elaborate sort of cunning, which consisted of vague doubts of 'something wrong' which doubts always being urged in an audible whisper, aided me rather than the reverse. My head was examined by Dr Hall, the wounds being covered with lint <u>and then the bandage produced in court wrapped round them</u>, which also I think dispels an illusion of Lord Coleridge's, who let the jury infer (without even putting a question to Mr Hall) that my wounds must have been mere scratches, as <u>the bandage was unstained!</u>

After leaving the hospital we returned to the Town Hall, and on the way there I accidentally found a cartridge in my trousers' pocket, which in desperation I dropped on the floor of the cab well underneath the seat. I was now presented to Mr Terry. I assumed the role of a deeply injured man, expressed my indignation, complained of my treatment, and was politely ushered out by him, but not before guessing that the two shabbily dressed men who took down my answers were detectives. However, without intending to wound the feelings of Holmes and Howland in the least, they neither appeared men likely to possess much penetration or smartness in the matter. At last I reached the station again, saw Mr Anscombe, and on being asked 'if I was much hurt' replied not as he swore saying 'I should think I was having <u>five or six bullets</u> in my head' but instead 'having five or six <u>wounds</u> in my head'. Here I was searched, of course nothing found beyond the watch, which I certainly did <u>not</u> tell Howland was mine. My sole reason for not letting Holmes see the pocket book was that I did not wish him to see the pawn tickets in it. We left for London. On the way up Mr Brown entered, talked with Holmes but I never heard a word about the body being found, never dreaming the hideous secret would be revealed so soon. In fact, I had a wild idea that possibly it might not be found for days, little thinking that tunnels were such thoroughfares as they evidently are.

On reaching Croydon I got Holmes to let me drive to Wallington as I did not wish anyone I knew in Croydon to see me in the terrible state I was in. The telegram received by the detective at E. Croydon made me still more anxious and when I reached Wallington I did my utmost to dispel any suspicions he might have of the truth by inviting him cordially in and offering to give him every assistance in my power. He took down my statement and then to my alarm asked me for the number of my watch. What followed is now so well known that I need not go over it again here. The instant the detective went I ran upstairs changed my clothes, said goodbye to my cousin, had something to eat and <u>fully twenty minutes</u> after Holmes had gone I went softly out at the front gate (there being no one in sight) and turned my back, weary and sick at heart, upon the dear old place for ever.

Conclusion

I walked from Wallington to London via Thornton Heath, Streatham and Kennington and arrived at the Sussex Hotel, Bouverie Street, Fleet Street about 1 a.m. where I slept for the night in the name of 'Lee'. All next day I was wandering about Victoria Park but at night I walked down to Blackfriars and slept at a coffee house near the bridge. The following day I spent on Blackheath and in Greenwich Park returning at night to London, throwing poor Mr Gold's watch over the middle arch of Blackfriars Bridge and sleeping at a coffee tavern near the Obelisk, and on Thursday I went to Mrs Bickers' where I remained until arrested on 8th July. The revolver I bought early in June at Vaughans' in the Strand. And the one found on the line has nothing to do with me whatever as mine was a six chambered one thrown out the rightside of Balcombe tunnel, and this I understand has only four chambers and was found near Earlswood. As to the hat found on the line I know nothing of it. I had only one 'low felt hat' and that besides being a very much better hat than the one produced at Maidstone, was worn by me the night I left Wallington, to be afterwards exchanged for a different sort of hat. I have one word to say in conclusion. I freely and sincerely, as I hope for mercy myself, forgive the ticket collector Franks the awful, deliberate misstatements he told at my trial. He knows and perhaps some day on his death bed he will confess it, that nearly every word of his evidence was incorrect. He never saw me get into Mr Gold's carriage at London Bridge, for I got in there at Croydon, and my ticket was never even examined by him but by the other collector North. What his motive was I cannot guess, but I sincerely trust that should the gentleman with whom I rode to Croydon ever see this, he will corroborate me in this particular. I never saw or heard of Mr Thomas Gold or any member of poor Mr Gold's family in my life, and no living soul but myself knew of my going to Brighton, or my intention in going.

I will not insult Mrs Gold by asking her to forgive me [last line crossed out] but I will however ask her to believe in the truth of what I have written and in my sincere and lasting repentance for the awful crime I have committed. Had I ten thousand lives I would give them willingly to bring poor Mr Gold once more to life. As that however is beyond my power I can only humbly confess my fault and seek forgiveness of Almighty God. I was very, very wicked to accuse myself of murdering poor Lieutenant Roper but I did so in the belief that it might postpone my execution, and now on the word of one whose life is ebbing fast I ask all who read this to believe me when I say that I had no knowledge or hand in the poor young officer's death.

On the very threshold of life I go to my grave with a hope that is ever getting stronger that even I may find in the mercy of Christ that peace and forgiveness to (which) I have been so long a stranger. Ambition (not one of the so called vices) has been my ruin on earth coupled with a fearful habit of deception, and I would earnestly pray that all parents would check the first lie in a child as they would the first symptom of a deadly disease. No one gets wicked all at once, they go step by step. The road daily becomes more easy, until at last they can go no further but find themselves engulfed for eternity in the <u>awful ruin</u> of everlasting death.

POSTSCRIPT

I am deeply sensible of the Christian charity of Mrs Gold for extending to me under such circumstances her past forgiveness for the incalculable wrong which I have done her and I sincerely regret that I am unable to give her any further information than I have done.

I wish this M.S. story of my life to be revised and examined by the Chaplain who is to have the sole right of saying whether it is to be published or no. If he thinks to have it published I should like him to act in the matter with Mr T. Clayton of Wallington, who would represent my relatives. In the event of the M.S. being published it must be printed in its entirety as it leaves the hands of the Chaplain, with the addition of a preface to it written by him. Should it be published all profits accruing from its sale are to be devoted to paying the cost of my defence.

Nov. 28 1881
Signed : Percy Mapleton

PART THREE

A PASSING BELL
FOR THE LIVING MAN

24

Tuesday, November 29th 1881.

After a windy night, the morning was beautiful, cloudless and spring like, as bright and mild as any day in May. A white frost enveloped the hills and hedgerows and the South Downs were bathed in a mist which gradually evaporated away. As it lifted, the sun shone brilliantly over the nearby valleys. On the 7 o'clock train from Brighton to Lewes passengers joked about Lefroy's fate and some expressed grave concern that there might be a last minute reprieve. Just as the train pulled into Lewes the sun lit up a new castellated building on the horizon above the town. It was situated on the spur of a hill to its west which overlooked a picturesque valley down which the eye could sweep as far as Newhaven.

'Has Marwood come over by this train?' passengers asked as they got out at the station.

They looked about for the well-known figure of the public executioner. Unbeknown to them, he was already at his place of work. In the distance they could see, ranged row above row, the glow of lights shining brightly from the prison, which was lit from wing to wing.

Strangely, by 8 o'clock not a solitary individual could be found by the prison gates. And Lewes itself was virtually deserted apart from those passengers who had travelled to be near the execution. The atmosphere was unusually calm and peaceful, all the more surprising because it was cattle and corn market day, which usually brought in a large influx of visitors. The reporters arrived. As they were not to be admitted until 8.30, they wandered down the quiet high street to distract themselves from their grisly task. But even there, portraits in shop windows of the sallow youth, who they had come to see die, met their uneasy eyes.

Slowly the journalists made their way up the hill to the grim battlements. More than one reflected on how little the exceptional brightness of the weather harmonised with the depressing nature of the proceedings. Still early, they ambled about the garden in front of the main building. Outside the walls a few children were playing, and a dozen adults stood about, including three policemen and two cab drivers. As the hour of execution approached, more police arrived to guard the outer gates and to patrol outside near the spot where the hanging was to take place.

At 8.30 precisely, a little wicket gate in the prison lodge opened and one by one, fourteen reporters passed inside. On entering, each was ushered into the waiting room and asked to sign a book. Once inside the prison all the pleasant surroundings of the countryside were gone. Huge walls now intervened between them and the Sussex Downs, although the blue sky above could occasionally be seen. Here and there a ray of sunshine penetrated the square which stood between the outer gates and the inner prison, but bars and bolts, the clanking of keys, and the noise of prison bells all militated against any feeling of enjoyment.

Surrounded by gloom and dullness, the small party were led to what was called the visiting committee's room. It was a snug apartment, warmly curtained, with crimson hangings, and with a roaring fire blazing in a large grate. But it was like the rest of the prison, barred with iron. The warder told them to wait until they were ready for them.

While waiting, some busied themselves by sitting at a long table and scribbling the first few lines of their reports. Others chatted in subdued tones. One enquired of the official of the door whether anyone would come and give the group the usual preliminary information, as had happened on previous occasions. He replied that they were under strict orders to give no information whatsoever.

From the window of the room they watched warders on the top of the outer wall busily engaged with a black flag and other officials rushing about. At length, a bell rang out a deep tenor note. It was a quarter to nine. And then silence. The suspense was broken by quick footsteps and the entry of the chief warder who enquired: 'Gentlemen, will you be good enough to walk this way?' With the sound of another doleful bell, the straggling line of newsmen passed down the steps of the gaol into a yard beyond. They passed more than one square, peering in vain for the scaffold at every entrance. Along these squares, by the cells, the heads of some of the prisoners could be seen peeping out to catch a glimpse of the procession whose route seemed terribly long and tedious. Suddenly, the chief warder stopped the cortege and warned them to be silent during the execution as 'you know, gentlemen, this is a solemn affair'.

They found themselves in a large irregular space which contained a row of celery trenches at one end. The space was bounded on one side by the end of the prison, and on the others by high walls. However, this was no ordinary space. For there, in the right hand corner facing the area where the vegetables were grown rose a couple of newly painted solid black posts. They were connected by a huge crosspiece from which dangled a staple and a long thick rope. As the rope swung lightly in the breeze it made a creaking sound which broke the eerie silence. Not ten yards away was a rude grave, dug in the chalky soil, with a heap of earth beside it, ready to be shovelled back in again. As they filed into the yard they were saluted one by one with a 'Good morning, gentlemen' by a diminutive man in a brown cloth suit with leather straps in his hand. It was Marwood. He was standing near the door leading to the courtyard waiting for the signal to enter the condemned cell. He told the journalists that the arrangements were 'excellent' and, gazing admiringly at the cross bar of black wood, said, 'That rope you see there, is made of Italian hemp two and a half inches round. I've hung nine with it, and it's the same I used yesterday in Manchester . . . The pit's all new, new brickwork you will see, and made on purpose.'

To Marwood, the whole thing seemed a triumph of art, and he moved backwards and forwards explaining the superiority of his design to his attentive audience: 'You see here, on the right of the gallows, facing it, is an iron lever, which when removed, releases the drop, which is formed by a heavy planked platform divided into two lengthways. When they fall they are held firmly by a spring, and so they don't swing to and fro.'

All the while the prison bell dismally tolled; a passing bell for the living man; the summons calling him to his fate. At length, a warder came bustling up, and with a bundle of keys in his hand, beckoned to Marwood, 'Ready for you'. With a complacent look, the hangman gathered up his tackle and disappeared up some steps which led to the condemned cell, leaving behind him the reporters fidgeting nervously.

During the night, Lefroy had turned two or three times from side to side, but had generally slept well. He awoke at six after being disturbed by the unlocking of cell doors. After dressing, he had a light breakfast of coffee, bread and butter and looked at his books for the last time. Moments later the chaplain began to administer the last rites and they had one last conversation.

At a quarter to nine the governor, the under-sheriff, and the chief warder entered his cell. He was still kneeling down in prayer with the chaplain. He rose and thanked all the officials for the kindness they had shown him. Marwood appeared and quickly passed a leather belt round Lefroy's body, fastened his elbows and wrist and pinioned his arms.

While he did so the young man asked:

'Do you think the rope will break?'

Those were Lefroy's last words.

'No, it will be quite safe,' replied Marwood.

Back in the yard the reporters were getting impatient. At three minutes to nine they heard a sound. A door leading into the yard opened. The eyes of the small group of witnesses instantly turned towards it. A procession slowly emerged, headed by the chaplain, who was reading the first sentence from the Church of England burial service. His loud clear voice resounded with startling distinctiveness through the high walled prison yard with the solemn and impressive exhortation, 'I am the

Resurrection and the Life'. He was followed by the governor and then Lefroy, unshaven and with his hair dishevelled. He was bareheaded and dressed in his own clothes; a shabby dark green tweed suit with no collar. His shirt front was open, exposing his long thin neck and narrow, hollow chest. He had the appearance of a prematurely worn old man. With his arms pinioned, he staggered rather than walked between two warders who hurried him along at a fast pace. Behind came Marwood, holding onto Lefroy's belt to steady him.

Along a narrow stone path through the courtyard they headed for a secluded triangle of the prison, chiefly used as an exercise yard for the prisoners. Hats were removed as it moved along. After a quick anxious glance at the Press, who were congregated to the left, Lefroy looked straight ahead, and seemed unaware of what was going on around him. The chaplain's words, rising and falling upon the ears of the spectators, were evidently lost on him, as he stumbled helplessly along. All the bravado witnessed in the dock at Maidstone had gone.

Marwood, never letting go of Lefroy's belt, several times pushed him forward as he got nearer and nearer the black wooden posts. When Cole read the words of the service giving promise of the Resurrection, Lefroy appeared to glance at him, the only indication of consciousness he showed. And thus the solemn cortege moved over the yard with the death bell still sounding its jarring and mournful notes above the rising tones of Cole's voice.

On reaching the scaffold, Lefroy hesitated for a moment – but it was only a moment – then stepped firmly onto the trapdoors before facing the small silent group of spectators. The fatal noose swung close to his head. The warders held him while Marwood fastened a broad leather strap around his legs and took a few seconds to adjust the noose to his neck. The swaying of Lefroy's body showed the nameless agony he was enduring. Next, Marwood took from his pocket a white glazed calico cap, and roughly drew it over Lefroy's trembling face. As he did so, the prisoner appeared to turn his eyes heavenwards and look at the sky intently for one moment. His lips moved as in prayer. He swayed again.

Marwood grasped Lefroy's hand firmly and then stepped backwards. Cole turned his back to the scaffold and moved off to about twenty feet to the right whilst the other officials remained in front. 'Lord have mercy upon us, Christ have mercy upon us,' he cried in trembling tones, without waiting for any response. The warders left Lefroy's side and Marwood placed his right hand on his shoulder. At the last word, and at exactly one minute to nine, the executioner slipped away from Lefroy and pulled the lever. The body dropped completely out of sight and fell with a heavy thud which was echoed by a murmur from the small crowd. The body had fallen 10 feet. Cole was the first to break the painful silence which ensued by crying 'Amen!' in a grave voice just as the body disappeared from view into the pit below. He then quietly closed his book.

As the drop fell, one warder signalled to another at the far end of the yard and the black flag was quickly run up over the entrance of the prison. A slight shout went up amongst the waiting crowd, which had grown to 200, including a dozen women. It was not known whether any of Lefroy's relatives were there.

Marwood looked down into the pit at the haze of steam rising from the corpse in the cold morning air. After a careful examination of the swinging figure and a glance at his watch, he walked quietly out of the quadrangle into the prison. He told the waiting reporters that Lefroy had died 'without a struggle'.

The doctor examined the dead man, followed by the reporters. No one actually descended into the pit. The body hung like a leaden weight and the white cap had slightly slipped in the fall. The whole head had been twisted round by the violence of the fall; the neck was very bruised and swollen; the face was discoloured; and the hands were convulsively jerked upwards. Lefroy had been so tightly pinioned that his wrists were bruised. The chief prison officials and reporters slowly dispersed, leaving the body suspended in the charge of a few of the warders.

At 10 o'clock, after the body had hung the usual hour, it was cut down by Marwood. Death notices were posted outside the prison walls and throughout the day were eagerly scanned by passers by. The proceedings were not over, however. A little after ten, the Press, prison officials, coroner and jurymen met in the committee room to determine how Percy Lefroy Mapleton 'now lying dead within the precincts of the gaol' had met his end.

The evidence was, of course, merely formal. The body was identified by the governor and the prison doctor added the gratuitous information that death had been caused by hanging. Lefroy's neck had been broken and his death was thought to have been instantaneous. The jury were taken to the infirmary, a large room containing three or four beds and a bath. There, on trestles and close by a door in an elm coffin, lay the body of the dead man with his boots still on. He had evidently been measured for his coffin while alive. Several of the jurors felt the face and hands which were still warm and indulged in sundry prods and pushes to satisfy their curiosity as to the physique of the dead man. The white cap and the pinion straps had been removed and there was some discoloration of the face. The features looked calm, and save for the abrasion on the neck and a slight breaking of the skin by the hangman's rope, he might have been mistaken for one asleep.

The viewing over, the jury returned to the room. Without comment they returned a formal verdict: 'Death was caused by hanging, in conformity with the Law'. The body was then buried by the prison works unit in quicklime, near the scaffold, in the plain wooden coffin which was drilled with holes so as to make any exhumation impossible. As the reporters filed out of the prison into the morning sunshine, each seemed to be profoundly shaken by what they had just witnessed.

Strangely, Lefroy had once written a poem called, 'What is Life?' The last verse asked:

> *'What is life?' the murderer cries*
> *As he sits in his prison cell,*
> *Chained like a dog; his last hope*
> *A speedy death from the hangman's rope.*
> *Mock echo, is this life?'*

25

It is difficult to assess the veracity of Lefroy's account of the murder, but the sequence of events (such as the throwing of various items out of the train window) was corroborated by the evidence produced at the trial. His claim that he never entered Gold's compartment until East Croydon was backed up by Williams' undermining of collector Franks' evidence. The guard in charge of the train, Thomas Watson, remembered seeing Mr Gold sitting all alone at that station. Lefroy later told the chaplain he believed that the man who acted as if 'he knew I came to murder him' was the same passenger who had almost left the train at Hassocks Gate when it had slowed down.

As for the role of the tempter whispering its hellish words, it seems to have been a dramatic expression of Lefroy's thoughts rather than an hallucination. After he throws Gold out of the carriage they rage uncontrollably in his mind: it would be surprising, though, not to feel some sort of mental instability after the unprovoked murder of an old man in a blood- spattered compartment.

Afterwards, Lefroy's fooling of all the railway officials and police at Brighton does beggar belief. However, it also demonstrates his ability to deceive, an ability which was never better illustrated than in his convincing Henry Bracy, an experienced actor who had toured in Australia, that he was an Australian. The policemen he fooled in Brighton were not novices, either. James Terry, the Brighton chief of police, had been in the force virtually all his working life and George Holmes was an experienced detective of 11 years' standing.

Lefroy admits in his autobiography that he was aware the officials felt something was wrong. At the inquiries, nearly all the railwaymen claimed they thought he had attempted suicide. But if they believed that, why did they not have him arrested, as it was a criminal offence? In reality, the testimony of the railway officials was rather confused throughout the inquest, magistrates' enquiry and the trial. More than one of them claimed to have spotted the gold watch in Lefroy's shoe. All in all their testimony often gave the impression of men trying to cover up a huge blunder. Possibly, their lethargic behaviour may have been affected by the tremendous heat of the day especially as summer uniforms had not yet been introduced for railway workers.

Lefroy was unlucky in one respect though, for the 2 o'clock express train on June 27th was *not* scheduled to stop at Preston Park. It had only been stopping there for a couple of weeks as an experiment for the tickets to be collected and the railway timetable had not yet been altered to include this change. Had the train not stopped and instead gone straight to Brighton, he might have had a slim chance of escaping amid the hustle and bustle of that much larger station.

Documents at the PRO placed in the public domain after the hundred-year rule make it clear there was never much chance of a reprieve for Lefroy. After receiving the petition for a postponement on the grounds of insanity, the Liberal home secretary, Sir William Harcourt, wrote a secret memo: 'This is the oft repeated case of an afterthought defence not set up at the trial or even suggested and at the last moment fired at the Secretary of State as a forlorn hope.'

Neither was he keen on the idea that the psychiatrists, Drs Forbes-Winslow and Winn, should conduct such an examination: 'Dr Winslow and Winn are the last persons to whom such an enquiry should be entrusted. I suggest Dr William Orange of Broadmoor Lunatic Asylum.'

In the end, Harcourt rejected the idea and, indeed, recommended that no reply should be sent to Lefroy's solicitor, Dutton, till the Saturday before the execution, thereby giving him little time to respond. Although Harcourt was a conservative when it came to capital and corporal punishment, he was a liberal over matters of civil liberties. While Lefroy was on the run he had turned down a request from Scotland Yard for permission to open his family's post. Why was Harcourt so reluctant to authorise a medical examination and postpone the execution? The truth was that Lefroy's 'escape' had caused enormous embarrassment to the authorities and made the police a figure of fun.

In the days leading up to the execution it appears that Lefroy may have broken down. Years later the psychiatrist employed by his family, Dr Forbes-Winslow, in his autobiography *Recollections of Forty Years*, recalled that 'information reached me from the precincts of the prison that Lefroy was "raving like a lunatic and foaming at the mouth". This information, I had reason to believe, as is usual in such cases, was suppressed by the authorities from the general public.'

The day after the execution, on the advice of the governor, the chaplain wrote to Captain Stofford, the prison commissioner, about the autobiography:

In my opinion it was written to assist in defraying the large and pecuniary outlay expanded in his defence from very limited means. The account was written day by day since his sentence with my full cognizance and the primary objects which he stated to me were:

First, that he might if possible during the short remainder of his life 'do some little good' by deterring others from the vices of his career.

Second, that he might do anything in his powers to correct the mock heroism which had by the public prints been cast around the case and might present it in a true and proper light to the public.

Third, that he might make the only reparations left to him by exonerating persons who he had implicated in his various frauds and deceptions, and also might clear up all uncertainty and misconceptions surrounding the murder of Mr Gold and give a truthful account of the circumstances of that awful crime and a heartfelt expression of his earnest contrition.

And lastly, as I have stated, afford any assistance he could to his friends whose means have been crippled for his sake.

I may say the tone of the manuscript bears out the above named intentions and that I shall be willing if the authorities see fit to exercise the revision requested by the criminal or to deal with the matter in any way they may decide.

Subsequent explanations given to me by him since the account was written would necessitate correction in some of the details for which reason the MS which I hold would not in its present form (unrevised) represent the <u>final</u> expression of the writer if sent for your perusal. The style of writing although characteristic would in my opinion require considerable modification before publication, not that it is, I am bound to say, in any sense improper.

If you can kindly afford me information to guide me in this matter I shall be extremely obliged.

Cole seems to have had some sympathy for Lefroy. Shortly after the execution, he told reporters he believed Lefroy 'on the whole, had been unfairly judged by the public' and that he was 'a strange mixture of good and bad and the victim of a bad upbringing'.

A week later, when Cole sent the manuscript with a covering letter to Stofford, he seems to have had a change of heart about its publication.

I send herewith the MS which, on considering a second time, I am bound to think, notwithstanding my desire to further the wishes of the writer as far as practicable, would not be suitable for publication, certainly as a whole.

Although the main purpose of the record was I believe good on his part, especially in the wish to assist his friends, I do not feel able to recommend its disclosure, nor can I vouch for the truth of any of its contents.

It is only just that I should add that the criminal constantly struggled against his inherent propensity to falsehood and was in his demeanour most humble, submissive and attentive from the time of his trial to his end, doing as much as his extraordinary character was I believe capable of both to realise his awful position and to prepare for another state. He had no fear of death itself.

One can only speculate whether the prison authorities pressurised Cole into changing his initial recommendation. The manuscript was sent to the home secretary, Sir William Harcourt, who passed it to his assistant, Liddell, attaching a message that, if it were not objectionable, it should be handed to the relatives to do what they pleased with it: 'We can have nothing to do with it.' After reading it, Liddell wrote back:

This in my opinion should go no further, certainly, not be published. It is a curious production written for effect and with considerable cunning and I believe no small part of lying. He carefully leaves out that part of his life between his schooldays and going to Australia and leaves it to be inferred that during that time he had met Miss Cameron whom he calls May Gordon and had received some promise from her whereas I don't believe she ever saw him in her life. Then there are many other persons whose names would be brought into unpleasant notoriety if they were published and several imputations at the trial. The whole story is high flown and emotional and impresses me rather with the action that vanity and a desire for notoriety more than a wish to write the naked truth dictated the production of it. If you agree I will lock this up in my secret cupboard.

Harcourt replied, 'I quite concur with your views on this miserable production. Should not see the light of day. Keep it locked up.'

It was placed under the hundred-year rule, and so Lefroy's family were never permitted to see the document. Neither were the Victorian public which had so eagerly followed the case.

Some time after the trial, two remarkable letters came into Montagu Williams' possession. One, dated October 17th 1881, was written by Lefroy and smuggled out of the prison. The other was discovered under Lefroy's mattress after his execution.

My Darling Annie,
I am getting this posted secretly by a true and kind friend, and I

trust you implicitly to do as I ask you. Dearest, should God permit a verdict of 'Guilty' to be returned, you know what my fate must be unless you prevent it, which you can do by assisting me in this way. Send me (concealed in a common meat pie, made in an oblong tin cheap dish) a saw file, six inches or so long, without a handle; place this at the bottom of the pie, embedded in under crust and gravy. And now, dearest, for the greater favour of the two. Send me, in the centre of a small cake, like your half-crown one, a tiny bottle of prussic acid, the smaller the better; this last you could, I believe, obtain from either Drs Green or Cressy for destroying a favourite cat. My darling, believe me when I say, as I hope for salvation, that this last should only be used the last night allowed me by the law to live, if it comes to that last extremity. Never, while a chance of life remained, would I use it, but only as a last resource. It would be no suicide in God's sight, I am sure.

Dearest, I trust this matter to you to aid me. I will face my trial as an innocent man should, and I believe God will restore me to you once more after this fearful lesson, but should He not, the file would give me a chance of escaping with life, while if both failed, I should still save myself from dying a felon's death undeserved. By packing these, as I say, carefully, sending with them a tin of milk, etc., no risk will be incurred, as my things are, comparatively speaking, never examined. Get them yourself soon, and relieve me, and direct them in a feigned hand, without any accompanying note. If you receive this safely, and will aid me, by return send a postcard, saying: 'Dearest P., Captain Lefroy has returned'. Send them by Friday morning at latest. If not P.A. get arsenic powder from Hart or other (or through Mrs B.); wrap up in three or four pieces of paper.

God bless you, darling. I trust you trust me. I can conceal several things about me in safety, your loving Percy.

The reply was in a woman's hand and because of its affectionate nature has always been accredited (by crime writers) to a girlfriend.

My Ever Dearest Percy,
I am writing this, hoping that Mr — will do me the great kindness of taking it to you, because I may not have another opportunity. First I must tell you that the delay about what you mentioned has happened through our being told that only two shops in London make them, but trust before you have this it will have arrived safely; if so, say in your next: 'The little basket with butter, etc., came safely.' As to the other thing, oh, my darling, my heart is almost torn with

the agony as to what to do about it. To think that I should be the means of putting you out of the world, or to think that it is I who leave you to an awful fate.

Darling, can a suicide repent? What is ANYTHING compared with our future happiness or misery? God can and WILL pardon ALL sins, the blackest and worst, if we are only sorry and believe in HIS power to save; but how about one that you have no time to be sorry in? In any case I could not get it from those you mention, nor the P.A. from Hart. If I were alone, no risk I incurred for YOUR SAKE I should think of for a moment; but it would be dreadful for the poor little ones were I taken from them for years, as I should surely be were it traced. I thought of Julia, but do not know whether it would be safe; say what you think. If the worst happens, shall we be allowed to see you once in a room? It would be time then.

Darling, YOU KNOW I would do ANYTHING for you I could, or that would not be BAD FOR YOU; but your soul is dearer and more precious than your body, and my one great, indeed, only comfort will be in looking forward to the time when WE SHALL MEET AGAIN; my love, if it were not for that hope, my misery would be UNBEARABLE. Oh, DO TURN to Him in this time of awful trouble; His arms are open to you. Whatever the verdict of the world may be, our dear mothers will rejoice to have you; ONLY confess all you have to confess to Him, who is able to save to the uttermost, and believe in His love. You know you have done many wrong things, and might have gone from bad to worse if this frightful calamity had not stopped you. I think certainly you have had some bad friends, and would be glad to know this – was it 'Lambton'? Are you shielding anybody?

My theory is this. Wanting means, the sight of the . . . was a great temptation, and unexpected resistance caused the rest; if this is correct, some time or other say: 'What you surmised in your last is, I fancy, correct,' or something like that, so that I may understand. My own dear one, I cannot fancy it prearranged; but of course I know something about the . . . that no one else does, and it is that in a great measure that fills me with such sickening dread and wretchedness for your sake. My darling, what did you want money *so much* for? Wouldn't it be a comfort to tell someone EVERYTHING you know? I would guard your honour as my own, and all would be safe with me. Think it over, and if what we dread happens, write me a few lines by MR — who, I know, will give it to me unopened. In any case your name and memory will ever be among those MOST LOVED and cherished by our dear little ones as well as ourselves, who know and love you now. Do you still wish for a likeness of V.C.?

One thing more. Has anything I have ever said, or done, or left unsaid or undone, helped you to do wrong? I feel bitterly that I have not been the friend I might have been in speaking more openly, etc., but I feared to hurt your feelings. Good-bye, my dearest, dearest Percy. PRAY WITHOUT CEASING that you may yet be restored to us in this world. God bless and comfort you.

Your ever loving and heart-broken Annie

I have tried through Smith to get a witness for third person, but as yet have failed. All I can do I will, you may be sure. My belief in your innocence is genuine, for I feel certain it was not intended. If by any merciful chance you succeeded with the implement, how should we know, to bring you things, etc.?

Lefroy's letter confirms his cellmate Foster's assertion that concealed objects were sometimes sent in to him. Prison security was far laxer for prisoners awaiting trial, but even if Lefroy did receive a file he was watched so closely by warders it would have been difficult for him to use it. The person who smuggled the letters in and out of the prison was probably Smith, Dutton's clerk.

It is now fairly obvious that the reply was written by his cousin, Anne Clayton, and it is clear – despite her postscript – that she knew something which convinced her he was guilty. It is also clear she believed someone else may have been involved. The two missing words in her letter were almost certainly 'money' and 'murder' and 'a likeness of V.C.' was undoubtedly Violet Cameron. Anne Clayton finishes the letter by virtually reproaching herself for her cousin's downfall.

Almost three weeks after his execution, Lefroy's letter to Violet Cameron – written three days before his death – appeared, rather surprisingly, in an obscure provincial newspaper, the *Kent Messenger*:

My dear Mrs Cameron,
A dying man is writing these lines to you, lines which no person here will read but the governor and the minister of religion, whose initials you will see on it, and in whose breast, I need hardly say, they will lie for ever undisclosed, and as a dying man I ask you to read them, and forgive this hand which so soon will be still and cold in the grave for penning them. When I first met and was introduced to you at the seaside in 1878, you were at Brighton,

when I was introduced to you in another name than my own. I loved you. Don't be angry. I was not always what I am now. Several times after I saw you, only to become more madly passionately fond of you. If I remember rightly you were only there a week, and when you left all the life and brightness of my life seemed to pass away. You had given me no encouragement, why should you, I was only a boy or a little more, and consequently you in the spring time of your fresh young life might naturally have thought had you given it a thought at all, that it was only a boy's admiration for a pretty girl. But it was not. It was that alone that has been the mainspring of my life ever since.

Hopeless, unrequited as it might be, it was an immense honest passion, and as such has saved me from many and many a sin I should otherwise have committed. From a distance I have watched your rise in your profession with mingled feelings of delight and at the same time of bitter despair. Delight at your well-deserved success, despair as every upward step you took widened the gulf between us. But all the same I have lived on with the vague hope of winning you in the end. Trying to do right for your sake, who knew nought of it.

And so you, with the world at your feet, loved by many and admired by all who knew you, and your brave unselfish life in your danger-beset profession, accept this last tribute, small and worthless though it may seem, of gratitude, aye and hopeless love, from one whose life is quickly closing in. You have always been my ideal of what a woman should be. Your face as I first saw it, is ever by my side, aye and will be to the bitter end, cheering me, comforting me, not with hopes that might have been, but what may be in the glorious future. God grant your life may continue as bright, as happy as it is now, and that your married life may be unsullied by any shock of grief or woe, and may your death be as happy as your life has been.

Violet, my darling, I call you so for the first and last time on earth – God bless you. My love for you will cease only with my life, and the dearest, most precious treasure I have in the world is a faded rose you carelessly gave to me nearly four years ago.

Percy Lefroy Mapleton

But did he really know her? We have to turn to Thomas Cole, the prison chaplain, for the answer:

On the day before his execution he informed me that the portion of the story inferring a personal acquaintance with 'May Gordon'

(Violet Cameron) was a 'romantic delusion' and that he had never spoken to her although he had adopted her as the goal of his ambitions! His friends seem to have been aware that some person of the kind was the object of all the scheming and deception of his life, and at the time he wrote to her from this prison I confess that I believed he really was acquainted with her.

(Letter dated 7/12/1880)

Violet Cameron as Lefroy first saw her, appearing as Germaine in *Les Cloches de Corneville*.

Violet Cameron appearing as Bettina in *La Mascotte* **at the time of Lefroy's trial.**

THEATRE.

Lessee and Manager . . . . MR. ALEX. HENDERSON.

Built from the Designs and under the Superintendence of

MR. THOMAS VERITY, F.R.I.B.A.

GENERAL CONTRACTORS	MESSRS. KIRK AND RANDALL, OF WOOLWICH.
FIRE-PROOF FLOORS	MESSRS. DENNETT AND INGLE.
STAGE FITTINGS	MR. LITTLEJOHNS.
GENERAL DECORATIONS	MR. E. W. BRADWELL.
UPHOLSTERY AND FURNITURE	SHOOLBRED & CO.

(Who have also Decorated and Fitted up the Principal Saloon.)

CARTON PIERRE DECORATION .. .. JACKSON & SONS.

At 8 o'clock, an entirely New and Original OPERA COMIQUE, in Three Acts, (the Latest Parisian Success, after CHIVOT and DURU), entitled

THE MASCOTTE.

Music by AUDRAN.

English Version by Messrs. H. B. FARNIE and R. REECE.

CONDUCTOR ... ... MONS. VAN BIENE.

All the Music of this Opera—the complete Vocal Score, the Pianoforte Edition, all the separate Songs and Arrangements for Dance Music—to be had in the Theatre, or of the Publishers, Messrs. BOOSEY & Co., 295, Regent Street, W.

COSTUMES		MONS. AND MDME. ALIAS.	
MACHINERY .. .. MR. LITTLEJOHN.	PROPERTIES .. .. MR. BRUNTON.		
FURNITURE .. .. J. LYONS & SON.	GAS .. .. MR. PURVIS.		
ASSISTANT STAGE MANAGER.. .. .. MR. E. T. STEYNE.			
CHORUS MISTRESS .. .. Mrs. JOHNSON.			

REFRESHMENT DEPARTMENT.

The elegant Saloons and Bars, fitted in the most improved and elaborate manner, and supplied with the very best refreshments, under the direction of the eminent American firm of BELLE and BOYD.

SPECIAL NOTICE.

The Box-office, Cloak-rooms, &c., are under the direct control of the Management.

Programme for the English version of La Mascotte at the Comedy Theatre in October, 1881, starring Violet Cameron and Henry Bracy.

CHARACTERS.

LAURENT XVII. ...	...	(Duke of Piombino)	... Mr. LIONEL BROUGH.
PIPPO	...	(A Shepherd)	... Mons. GAILLARD.
PRINCE FRITELLINI	...	(Crown Prince of Pisa)	... Mr. HENRY BRACY.
ROCCO	...	(A Farmer)	... Mr. T. P. HAYNES.
MATHEO	...	(An Innkeeper)	... Mr. W. BUNCH.
PARAFANTE ...	...	(A Sergeant)	... Mr. GORDON.
BIANCA }			Miss ADA WILSON.
TITO } ...	...	(Bohemians)	... Miss K. ABRAHAMS.
GUISEPPE ...	...	(A Peasant)	... Mr. C. HUNT.
PRINCESS FIAMMETTA ...		(Laurent's Daughter)	... Miss ST. QUINTEN.
BETTINA ...		(A Country Girl—" The Mascotte")	Miss VIOLET CAMERON.

ANGELO		Miss CLARA GRAHAM.	PAOLA		Miss M. DOUGLAS.
LUIGI		Miss ANNIE DEACON.	FRANCESCA		Miss MADGE MILTON.
BEPPO	The Royal Pages.	Miss KATE PERCIVAL.	ANTONIA	Maids of Honour.	Miss C. GARDINER.
CARLO		Miss CALLAWAY.	ZANETTA		Miss BESSIE BELL.
LEONE		Miss ELISE WARD.	ANITA		Miss CLAYTON.
PEDRO		Miss E. DOUGLAS.	ELVIRA		Miss F. YOUNG.

FINELLA ...	...	(A Bohemian) ...	... Miss EMILY ASH.
MARCO ...	...	(A Bohemian) ...	Miss NELLIE HODGES.

Courtiers, Peasants, and Soldiers, Messrs. MORGANTI, PERRY, REEVES, VAUGHAN, and WILKINSON. Mesdames L. and M. BEAUFORT, BEAUMONT, BELL, HOWE, JACKSON, LANCASTER, LYTTON, NELSON, VICKMORE, HAMILTON, CHAPMAN, TOLBY, POWELL, HUDSON, RUSSELL, DRUMMOND, MELVILLE, and ST. ROY.

Act I.—"ROCCO'S HOMESTEAD."
(W. PERKINS.)

AGRICULTURAL DISTRESS. THE MASCOTTE TURNS UP.

Act II.—"PALACE OF PIOMBINO."
(T. E. RYAN.)

GOOD TIMES. THE MASCOTTE POLICY A GREAT SUCCESS.

Act III.—"BIVOUAC IN THE FOREST."
(T. W. GRIEVE.)

STRATEGY. DESTINY OF THE MASCOTTE.

The whole produced under the Direction of Mr. H. B. FARNIE.

Morning Performance every Saturday at Two o'Clock. Doors open at 1.30.

STAGE MANAGER... ... ... Mr. LIONEL BROUGH.

ACTING MANAGER ... ... Mr. R. D'ALBERTSON.

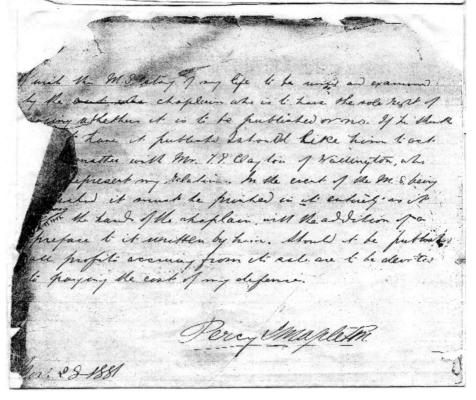

Examples of Lefroy's handwriting. At the end of his preface (above) he signs himself Percy Lefroy Mapleton, but at the foot of his autobiography he omits the name that made him infamous.

Chamber of horrors: Lefroy's waxen image confronted visitors to Madame Tassauds in London for many years. (Madame Tussads Archives, London)

Conclusion

The horrific act of June 27th 1881, which left an elderly, innocent man bleeding to death in the damp, inhospitable darkness of the Balcombe tunnel – a spine-chilling tomb – shocked the whole of British society. There is no doubt that Lefroy committed the murder, but there is great doubt about his sanity. His autobiography – now lying in the National Archives – is, of course, self absorbing and could evoke the feeling of someone trying to make literary capital out of their own experiences. But read as an account of a stressed mind suffering a mental disturbance it looks different. It shows a perceptive analysis of his own downfall.

No one can read Lefroy's terrifying account of the murder and not deduce that by the time he entered that train he had descended into some form of madness. And if his defence counsel had been able to tell the court that the crime had been committed in furtherance of efforts to declare his love for a music hall actress he had never met, who then would have doubted his insanity?

Forbes-Winslow thought Lefroy 'was not only insane, but was subject to outbursts of homicidal impulse'. He also believed that his lies were delusions, the result of a diseased mind. But delusion means false belief not amenable to correction by reason. Lefroy admitted to being a life-long liar and conman, but in his later confession directed to the chaplain he showed, when he wished, that he was a stickler for accuracy – the change of compartments at Croydon, for instance, and his correction of witnesses' statements. One imagines, given the opportunity and faced with the disparity, that he would have admitted as fabrication the lock of hair when on the point of suicide in Australia, when it is clear he had never met 'May Gordon'. It was in his effort to achieve such a meeting through Bracy that he got involved in his last desperate act.

Lefroy was clearly driven. Here was a romantic liar, a gentle, sentimental poseur with a histrionic literary flair who came to focus his Walter Mitty fantasy on a hopeless unrequited love. He was gripped by this 'overvalued idea'. Like any obsession or compulsion, this can have as much driving force as any delusion. An eminent psychiatrist today wonders whether he may have been distancing himself from unacceptable feelings towards Frank Seale, whom he calls 'darling' in his last letter. Or perhaps it was just a demonstration of his love for a person who had been like a father and brother to him. Anyhow, in the event 'Lester's' bounced cheque collapsed his financial house of cards and he could not face public failure and derision. Once launched on his desperate plan to kill for some money, how far could he be deemed responsible? It is difficult to say.

Lefroy clearly had psychopathic tendencies. Perhaps it is more accurate to say that he had a lifelong personality disorder in which, as the chaplain said, 'he constantly struggled against his inherent propensity to falsehood'. In the light of his confession that he had never ever spoken to Violet Cameron one can only guess what form his actual contact with her was. How often had he waited by stage doors for a glimpse of her? How often had he sat watching her from the stalls with a ticket purchased from a pawned item of clothing or appeared at the stage door with flowers purchased on borrowed money? Lefroy's relationship with Violet Cameron became a figment of his imagination; a shadow of the relationship he had with the two real people he loved: Frank Seale and Anne Clayton.

Lefroy's autobiography revealed a gentle, loving complex character and in many ways is a heartfelt plea for understanding, not justification. One can only speculate how much his father's neglect affected his future behaviour. Lefroy's disappointment in him is best illustrated by his invention of fictitious famous relatives at the expense of someone he could have justly boasted about, the heroic figure of a young Staff Commander Henry Mapleton and his Arctic adventures. It wasn't as if he knew nothing about his father's exploits: sometimes he pawned items in the name of one of the boats he had rescued from the Arctic ice, *William Lee*.

In his conclusion he admits that 'ambition . . . has been my ruin on earth coupled with a fearful habit of deception'. We can only speculate whether, as Cole wrote, Violet Cameron really was 'the object of all the scheming and deception of his life' and if it was the pursuit of this hopeless love and the extravagance involved which created the circumstances leading to the murder. Perhaps this was the answer to Anne Clayton's desperate demand of him in her secret letter: 'My darling, why did you need money <u>so much</u>?'

Lefroy sold everything he had to ingratiate himself with the world of the theatre. His abject poverty, clearly demonstrated during the trial, contrasted strongly with the glittering success he must have dreamed of obtaining in that world. Or was it perhaps his chronic ill health – confirmed by his family and prison cellmate Foster – that foretold a short life and made him in such a hurry for fame and fortune?

Lefroy loved the theatre and literature, and through them hoped to fulfil his hopes and fantasies. And they were so nearly in his grasp, for he truly possessed some literary talent for one so young. What an irony it was that his life itself, became true theatre – a tragic drama – and that in a perverted way he did achieve the fame he so craved, ending up as a notorious exhibit at Madame Tussauds. At the last, when he was in the 'Dark Valley of the Shadow of Death', he repented and sought redemption. In the end, as Cole said at the time, he had no fear of death itself.

Postscript

Unfortunately the vast majority of papers held at the Public Records Office about the Lefroy case were destroyed. This may have been because they were insignificant: on the other hand they may have revealed details which the Home Office decided were best kept secret. There is no mention of the whereabouts of the razor and revolver used in the murder or of Mr Gold's watch. In the surviving papers there is also little about Lieutenant Roper, and to this day his murder remains unsolved.

The true identity of one of the men who visited Scotland Yard on the evening of Lefroy's arrest was not revealed until more than a hundred years later, when the Public Records Office released records about the case. His name was Mr Mugford and he worked at the same city firm as Frank Seale. According to police records, it was Mugford whom Mrs Bickers' daughter, Clara, saw in connection with the telegram and who, putting two and two together, concluded she was describing the wanted man. He then went with an unidentified friend to the police. Mugford received £100 of the reward money. Mrs Bickers, who wrote several letters to the Home Office begging for a large payment, received only £15 for her unintentional role in Lefroy's capture. Jarvis and Swanson, the police inspectors, were each given £5.

Immediately after the murder, the railway company had issued a statement declaring that the communication cord had been in good working order, but the statement had been of small comfort to the travelling public who were worried that even if the victim of a sudden attack managed to reach the alarm, the crew might not hear it above the din created by the engine. Eight years after Gold had embarked on his fatal journey, a new system was introduced, whereby a passenger could personally bring the train to an automatic halt.

The murder had a devastating effect on Lefroy's family. The Claytons were forced to move, and they and Frank Seale disappeared into obscurity. Cathcart Road was soon renamed Clarendon in order to disguise its infamous past, and Mrs Clayton's house was eventually destroyed by a bomb during the second world war. Lefroy's younger sister, Julia Mapleton, also faded from view. His older sister, Mary Brickwood, who was separated from her husband, emigrated to Australia with her six children immediately after the execution. There she established a hospital in Bundaberg, Queensland: today three of her great granddaughters are living in Australia and America.

The scandal involving 'Percy' was always a great family secret and one of them remembers 'various whispers in my grandparents' kitchen . . . none of the family wanted to talk about it', and locked cupboards with press cuttings.

Lefroy's landlady in Stepney, Mrs Bickers, also moved to another part of London because of the number of ghoulish sightseers who had besieged her home after his capture. One of the officers who arrested him, Donald Swanson, a few years later led the Jack the Ripper enquiry. Lefroy's solicitor, Mr Dutton, continued to insist that Lefroy was 'as mad as mad could be'. He also revealed that when he had asked Lefroy what he meant by his defiant words to the jury, he had simply replied 'I couldn't help it.'

Montagu Williams, Lefroy's lawyer, became a highly successful defence barrister and was later knighted for his work as a magistrate in campaigning against 'immoral' lodging houses in the East End in the wake of the Ripper killings. Less fortunate was the public hangman, William Marwood, who after the execution had told people that if he had not held Lefroy by the belt 'he would have given me a run around the yard'. A couple of years later the Home Office received complaints that Marwood had held 'receptions' at a pub before an execution and had exhibited the rope he would use. Soon afterwards he caught pneumonia while 'on duty' and died to little public mourning.

There is an irony here. Through the internet I discovered that 21 years before Lefroy's execution, the writer Mary Elizabeth Braddon had written a thriller called *The Trail of the Serpent* – the title used by Lefroy for one of his chapters. It is the tale of a murder. In the story the murderer feigns madness at his trial and is committed to a lunatic asylum. The murderer's name was Marwood.

Thirty years after Lefroy's execution, the psychiatrist Forbes-Winslow had still not changed his opinion:

> It was a popular murder, if I may use the expression – one in which, from the fact of the murder taking place in a railway train and one to which anyone might be subjected, the public thought that an example should be made.
>
> If ever there was a case in which the plea of irresponsibility should have been raised it was in the case of Lefroy. . . I am very strongly of the opinion that it would have been to the interest of intelligence, humanity, science, civilisation, Christianity and justice if a deaf ear had not been turned to the prayer of the unhappy man's family and medical petitioners, simply begging that the Home Secretary would grant them an enquiry into the mental

condition of the youth standing on the precipice of his fate. We asked no more than this, and were refused.

James Terry, the chief constable of Brighton, finally retired from his office in 1893 and became a local councillor. At his retirement dinner many paid tribute to his 'modest, retiring nature; his unvarying politeness to people; his genial, jovial disposition and kindly smile'. But the whole occasion was rather spoilt by one councillor standing up and calling him 'the most impotent man they had in the force'. Some excuse was found to retire Detective Sergeant George Holmes early: it was ironic that several years later Sir Arthur Conan Doyle should choose the surname of the unfortunate detective for his own highly successful sleuth. Rev. Thomas Cole retired at the turn of the century. And Henry Bracy, the actor whom Lefroy had liked so much, eventually emigrated to Australia.

Mr Gold's wife, Lydia, who had acted with such great dignity throughout the trial and indeed throughout the whole trauma, died in 1910 at the age of 86. She had chosen to remain at the house round the corner from Preston Park Station after her husband's death. Her own demise was barely recorded in the local press.

Perhaps, of all the people involved in the story, Violet Cameron's fate is the most interesting. Though still married, a few years after Lefroy's execution Violet had a very public affair with Lord Lonsdale, one of the richest men in England, famous for his extravagance and high living. He was also, according to Edward V11, the 'greatest liar in the Kingdom'. How ironic it was that Violet should fall in love with a person who, like Lefroy, had such a propensity for the untruth.

After she met Lonsdale, she started the Violet Cameron Operatic Company but the real manager and the financial backer was Lonsdale. He used to accompany her everywhere on tour. Once, after a performance in Newcastle, she returned with him to his hotel, where they were confronted by her furious husband. Lonsdale, who was a strong man, threw him out of her sitting room. The husband sued him for assault. Lonsdale was fined and the affair was blazoned across every newspaper in the land. It sparked off a series of petitions and cross-petitions between Violet and her husband; she suing for protection, he petitioning for divorce.

Things came to a head in 1886 in New York where she was touring. Both her husband and Lonsdale arrived in the city on the same day but by different ocean liners. After she moved into Lonsdale's hotel – although they had separate rooms – there was another angry confrontation which ended with her husband being jailed for threatening her. On her first performance there the audience was almost entirely made up of men and there was a strong police presence. The tour ended in farce with the seven month schedule being cut to seven weeks. When she got back to England she sued for divorce on the grounds of cruelty and slander. During the divorce case, which went to court, it transpired that Violet Cameron was carrying Lonsdale's child, and he was named as co-respondent.

After they were separated, however, her husband continued to stalk and pester her for money. He threatened to disfigure, stab and even shoot Violet and in her own words 'tried to assault me wherever I went'. She was in fear of her life. He would invade her dressing room and on one occasion the other actors refused to go on the stage unless he was evicted from the theatre. It took four men to throw him out and led to the performance being delayed.

Back in London, Lonsdale and Violet moved quite openly into a house in Hampstead, where they lived under the name of Mr and Mrs Thompson – Thompson was Violet's maiden name. But her husband continued to harass her. He often came round drunk and smashed the windows of the house and rang the doorbell for hours. As a result, Violet Cameron was close to a nervous breakdown: she had fainting fits and for a couple of years was unable to perform to the standard she had worked so hard to achieve.

This was all too much for Queen Victoria, who discreetly let it be known that she expected Lonsdale to leave the country until the scandal died down. He had no choice but to go. He quickly managed to organise a convenient expedition to the Arctic. During the expedition Violet kept in correspondence with him through his personal secretary. The 'exploration' lasted a year, and when Lonsdale returned to England he was greeted as a national hero. He also returned to his wife.

Thereafter, Violet's only contact with him was through his secretary, mainly in respect of their child's maintenance. In her letters to him she occasionally mentioned the name of Henry Bracy, confirming her obvious friendship with him. During her affair with Lonsdale and for many years afterwards the press continued to speak of Violet's relationship with Lefroy as if it were a fact.

When she had starred in *La Mascotte*, every night one of her co-stars, Lionel Brough, had said to her two lines which became so prophetically true in her own life:

> *If she loves whom she shall wed*
> *Then the Mascotte's power is dead.*

Her association with Lonsdale did her career no good at all. She stopped performing for a while in the early 1890s after appearing in a disastrous musical called *Miami*. She was lured back to the stage in 1903 to appear in a London show called *The School Girl* at the Prince of Wales Theatre. It lasted almost a year. Then she retired at the relatively young age of forty and went to live in Worthing. She died there on October 25th 1919 after a short illness. She was 56. Her obituaries reported that she had suffered a very unhappy marriage.

How strange it is that Lefroy, in his autobiography, had imagined a lord to be his rival in love for Violet; a lord who he feared would bring scandal and disgrace to her name. Lefroy had anticipated a real event several years before it had actually occurred. Both Lefroy and Lonsdale, in their own way, pursued theatrical aims as a means of wooing Violet Cameron and both lost money in the attempt. In Lefroy's case he also lost something far more precious: his life.

It is ironic that after his death some magazines, in the light of his notoriety, published some of his stories. Just before Lefroy's execution, another writer wrote:

> With regard to his literary ability, at which so much sneering had been indulged in, as a writer of some slight reputation, I can, in common with more than one editor of undoubted judgement, assert that, considering his extreme youth, he displayed a power and undoubted dramatic fire. His pantomime at Croydon was stated to be good; his story *Two Boxing Nights** was, I know, very good; and the little sketch now being published, *Released in Death*, is most certainly not unwanting in merit.

A waxworks model of Lefroy was on public display at Madame Taussauds from 1881 until 1997 when it was finally removed and melted down. Reputedly, the execution beam is still on display there. And an elderly woman who lives near Lewes recently told me that when she was a young girl she used to hear her mother singing:

Who killed Mr Gold in a railway carriage? Lefroy! Lefroy!

Today, in a cemetery on the periphery of Brighton, lies the unmarked grave of Frederick Isaac Gold and his wife. Five miles away lies another

---

* Reproduced as Appendix 2 on page 180

unmarked grave in a rough piece of ground between the north-east wall and an inner high steel fence inside Lewes Prison. There, Percy Lefroy Mapleton was buried in:

Only a stretch of mud and sand
By the hideous prison-wall,
And a little heap of burning lime,
That the man should have his pall,

Deep down below a prison-yard,
Naked for greater shame,
He lies, with fetters on each foot,
Wrapt in a sheet of flame!

And all the while the burning lime
Eats flesh and bone away,
It eats the brittle bone by night,
And the soft flesh by day,
It eats the flesh and bone by turns,
But it eats the heart away.

Oscar Wilde, 'The Ballad of Reading Gaol'

Both graves serve as a memorial to the tragic events of June 27th 1881.

Appendix 1

Scene: A railway platform. Policemen assembled. An inspector arrives and exchanges greetings. He sings, accompanying himself softly on the rattle:

Insp:
>   Doubt, we know, is from the devil,
>   Let us thrust its lures aside;
>   Constables who think no evil
>   Ever have been England's pride.

All (*enthusiastically*)
>   Ay! Away with base suspicion,
>   And with thoughts that wrong mankind!
>   Ill it were in our position
>   To indulge a cynic mind.

(*A train enters the station. They approach it*)

Insp.
>   See from yonder railway carriage
>   Who is emerging, pray,
>   In a plight 'twould scarce disparage
>   To describe as disarray?
>
>   Why! His face and hands are gory,
>   And exhausted he appears!
>   Stranger, pour your moving story
>   In our sympathetic ears.

(*He pours it*)
>   Ah, most startling! Ah, most thrilling!
>   Of romance 'tis strangely full!
>   Aged merchant – missing villain –
>   Countryman and cock-and-bull!

Insp.(*after a pause*)
>   Yet I fain would ask you, stranger,
>   How – but, no, this will not do;
>   Mutual trust it might endanger –
>   Who am I to question you?

All (*approvingly*)
>   Who, indeed? Avaunt, suspicion!

Down, ye thoughts that wrong mankind!
Ill befits it our position
To indulge a cynic mind.
(*Another pause, during which they eye the stranger closely*)
Insp. (*after a struggle with himself*).

Pardon, Sir, the strong desire I
Vainly labour to restrain;
But th' old Adam of inquiry
Rises in my breast again.

Tell me (thus a weakness lingers!)
How and when you tore your coat;
And are those not marks of fingers
That I see upon your throat?

Where's your collar? Where's your necktie?
Where – but why the questions press?
If your *mens* be *conscia recti*
What's a collar more or less?

All.

What indeed! Away suspicion!
Get thee, Satan's child, behind!
Let us each in his position
Shun that curse – a cynic mind!
(*Yet another pause. They still continue eyeing the stranger*)
Insp. (*diffidently*).

I despise the art of angling
For disclosures – mean pursuit!
But . . . I notice something dangling
(Not a bootlace) from your boot.

Ha! A watch-chain! I declare, it
Seems a funny place to – eh?
What! 'The way you always wear it?'
Say no more! Forgive me, pray!

True-born Britons never heed 'em.
Casual trifles such as these;
Heirs to centuries of freedom
Wear their watch-chains how they please.

All (*proudly*)

> True! Away then, vile suspicion!
> Spurn we thoughts that wrong mankind!
> Base it were in our position
> To indulge a cynic mind.

Insp.

> Now farewell! The word may grieve us
> Yet at last we must dismiss
> Dearest friends; but ere you leave us
> Gentle stranger, tell me this:
>
> Since we may your kind assistance
> Need to trace this dreadful crime -
> Are you going any distance?
> Or for any length of time?
>
> 'Just a week of foreign travel.'
> Thanks! Then we may count on you
> After that to help unravel
> This dark mystery! Adieu!

(*Stranger embraces the police beginning with the Inspector;then enters a continental train. They watch it moving from the station until it is lost to view*).

Insp. and chorus:

> Speed thee, speed thee, o'er the billow!
> I/We will not believe thee vile
> Smooth, O smooth is strewn the pillow
> Under heads that know no guile.
>
> Doubt, I/We feel, is from the devil
> I will/Let us thrust its lures aside.
> Constables that think no evil
> Ever have been England's pride.

(Extract from satirical poem HONI SOIT QUI MAL Y PENSE in *St James Gazette* 30/6/1881)

Appendix 2

TWO BOXING NIGHTS
by Percy Mapleton

Christmas time! There was no doubt about it. Everything and everybody savoured of it. The light of Christmas fires shone through and gleamed behind closely-curtained windows, with merry leaps, sending showers of golden sparks up dark chimneys, to emerge more bright and dazzling than ever in the clear, frosty air, like fleeting souls hastening through the gloom and cares of life to shine in higher regions.

"Christmas!" cried the bells, as they pealed softly through the still night air; "Christmas! merry Christmas! – Christmas! merry Christmas!" so merrily and cheerily that he must have been a man of stony heart who did not echo it, too, from sheer sympathy. Christmas! murmured the dark river, as it lapped against the buttresses of the old stone bridge, and then sped away with many a secret in its gloomy bosom to the sea, where, in company with many others of its race, it murmured still of Christmas; and "Christmas time!" pleaded the inebriated gentlemen when questioned by a stern policeman as to why they were sitting in frozen gutters at midnight. For that one day a sort of universal truce seemed to be established. Creditors forgot their debtors, debtors forgot their creditors; wives forgot to scold, husbands to abuse, and young husbands forgot their mothers-in-law, which was, perhaps, hardest of all. Conservatives and Liberals, Churchmen and Dissenters, "old boy'd" and "old fellow'd" each other to their heart's content, and the plea for all was – Christmas! But when the world got up next day, what a change was to be seen! Closed blinds, no church bells, shops shut – just as if every one was ashamed of his or her last night's festivity.

There wasn't much going on indoors today, for it was Boxing Day – that day sacred to Christmas boxes, bills, and last, but by no means least, pantomimes. And to go to one of these last the children were mad with hope long deferred. Papa and mamma affected not to like or care for such trivial amusements at all, but the children – sly dogs, those children! – knew that when once within the cosy recesses of that lovely private box no one would cry "bravo" more loudly, or clap his hands more vehemently, than papa. And what a lot of pantomimes there were, too! Just look at all the various hoardings: Robinson Crusoe, Jack the Giant-killer, Aladdin, and many other well-known stories had been made to contribute to the common good. But first and foremost among the brightly-coloured bills was one that informed the reader "that on Boxing Night would be produced at the Rotunda Theatre" the grand Christmas pantomime, Jack and the Beanstalk. Then followed the list of characters, scenery, etc., and at the end, in large letters, "Clown – Jolly Joe Jeffs".

The Rotunda must have been a well-known theatre for pantomime, for that night it was crammed from floor to ceiling. Everything had gone off without a hitch. The music was pretty, the scenery magnificent, and the grand ballet had been pronounced by the crutch-and-toothpick genius in the stalls to be "splendid", and by an old lady in the pit to be "beastly".

And now, out of breath with honest laughter, warm, thirsty, and packed like sardines in a box, the great audience sat anxiously awaiting for the "grandest transformation scene ever attempted at the Rotunda", vide bills. If there was excitement in front, so there was behind. Every one busy, excited, and nervous, the manager and stage-manager not being by any means in that happy condition described by the immortal Mrs Jarley as "Cool, calm, and classical."

Inside one of the principal dressing rooms was a man, clad in a clown's dress, pacing moodily up and down, and listening with feverish impatience for a footstep which never came. It was Joe Jeffs, and the person he was waiting for was his wife. And she was a wife worth waiting for, too. Young, pretty, and loving. Nellie Raynor, then only – and indeed, up to within a week or so of the present time – a ballet girl at a West End theatre, had brought some new joy and life to honest, hard-working Joe Jeffs, who, though nearly fifteen years her senior, loved her with a strong and passionate love, and would cheerfully have laid down his life if it had been necessary to save her from harm. And this winter, when Nellie, through her husband's influence, got engaged at the Rotunda as columbine, Joe Jeffs thought that his cup of happiness was full to the brim.

A knock at the door. "Come in," cried the clown. Mr Flies, the stage-manager entered. Flies was a little short man, with a round red face, with very short black hair, so short that it always stood on end, as if each hair was desirous of looking over its neighbour's head.

"I'm very sorry, Mr Flies," said the clown, humbly, "very sorry, but Nellie told me tonight she wasn't well, and would lie down for a bit, and would come later on. I sent a boy to our place some time ago, and she must be here in a minute."

"Minute!" roared Mr Flies, "what's the good of a minute? I – who the devil's that?" as a hand was laid on his arm.

It was the harlequin, in the bills Roberto Taylori, out of them, Bob Taylor, an old friend of the clown's.

"I've got an idea," said the harlequin, giving a kindly unseen nod to his friend. "Say a few words to the public, and let my girl Bella go on for the part tonight; she's about Mrs Jeffs' size, and I've taught her the trip long ago."

Miss Bella Taylori was in the front row of the ballet, consequently could dance well and look pretty; but, best of all, was there on the spot, so to speak. The stage-manager didn't take long to make up his mind.

"Bob," he said to the harlequin, "You're a brick. The very thing. Get the girl dressed at once, and I'll get the guv'nor to speak to them." Them being the audience, who were now in a state of noisy impatience. Mr Flies hurried off.

"Tell your missus it's all right old man," said the friendly harlequin, as he hurried away.

The clown was about to reply, when a light footstep was heard approaching. A happy smile lighted up his face. "At last," he said, with a sigh of relief, as the footsteps neared the door. Quickly he turned the handle and threw it wide open, but only to start back with a cry of disappointment, for the newcomer was not his wife, but the boy he had sent an hour previously. "Well," cried the clown, "what did she say?"

The boy shook his head stolidly.

"I didn't see her, sir," he said; "only the landlady, and she give me this." The clown held out his hand, and into it the boy put a tiny note, on which was written, in a woman's hand, "To be given to my husband."

"You can go," said Joe Jeffs in a voice which was so hoarse and strange that for a moment it startled the lad. When the door was again closed, the clown looked at the tiny missive. Was she frightened that he would be angry with her for remaining so long behind the time, and so did not care to come at all, but wrote instead? That must be it. With trembling hands he hastily tore it open, and read: "Husband, goodbye; I shall never see you any more. I am going away with someone that loves me very much. You were always too good for me. May God forgive your poor lost Nellie." Nothing more. Only an old, old story, with a vulgar clown and his wife as hero and heroine.

Joe Jeffs raised his head. Was it paint alone that gave that awful deathly look to his face and fixed glassy eyes? Was it clowning that caused the strong man's hands to shake as if he were suffering from the palsy? And, above all, was it art or nature which made that bitter cry of agony arise from the uttermost depths of a broken heart?

At that moment the call-boy's shrill voice was heard. "Mr Jeffs, the stage waits!" Mechanically the clown reeled to the door and opened it, down the narrow, dark passage, and staggered through the wing on to the brilliantly-lighted stage, and then in a voice more resembling the croak of a raven than the utterance of a human being, gave vent to the time-honoured utterance, "Here we are again!"

How the house roared at the strange voice and staggering gait! Such quiet humour!" So dry, very dry! And then, after such a capital commencement, the great audience settled down with keen anticipation for the fun that was to come. And come it did. With what zest did Jolly Joe Jeffs trip up the policeman, steal the sausages, and go through the hundred and one odd tricks which go to make up the sum total of a harlequinade! The gods were in one continual roar; and even the stalls and circles were mildly excited, while as for the pit, the opinion of that black, seething mass of humanity may be briefly summed up in the words of an excited old gentleman, who, carried away by his enthusiasm, flung his neighbour's hat into the air, crying, "splendid, sir, splendid! Grimaldi was a fool to Jolly Joe!" And tumbling, grimacing, tripping up, now dancing on a spade, a minute later cracking sly jokes, the clown went through it. Only the clown, though, for God's beautiful creation – man – was gone. When his poor, aching head swam for a moment, and he fell heavily to the ground, what a shout went up! Droll fellow, that Jeffs – very droll, and their laughter reached its culminating point when, during a hornpipe by the pretty columbine, two large tears stole down the clown's painted face, as he, in burlesque fashion, attempted to imitate it. "He's a-crying with laughter!" roared the excited gallery, and they cheered him to the echo for entering so heartily into the spirit of the thing. At last the end came. One last wild trick, clouds of smoke from the coloured fires, a last mad rally, and, amidst tremendous applause, the pantomime was over. As the band commenced to play the National Anthem, Jolly Joe Jeffs staggered off the stage, as he had staggered on. Ere he could reach his dressing-room two men stopped him. One was Mr Flies, the other Mortimer, the Manager. "My boy," said the latter, taking him by both hands, and shaking them warmly, "you've surpassed yourself. If only your wife could have seen you!" That was enough. For a minute Jolly Joe stood erect, and then with a wild, gasping cry, fell heavily to the ground. The clown was gone, but the man was there.

NIGHT THE SECOND

Ten years rolled by. Ten long, weary years they had been to Joe Jeffs, who had never given up the search for his lost darling. A few weeks after his great loss an old relative had died, leaving him a small annuity. On this he had lived, or rather existed, wandering aimlessly about the country in the hope of one day finding his wife, whom in spite of all, he loved as fondly as ever.

And this Boxing Night, he was walking down the little High Street of Milford, weary, hopeless, and sick at heart, to all appearance a bent, careworn, old man, a mere wreck of the merry fellow who ten years before had made a great theatre resound with peals of laughter at his drollery. Quickly the clown walked on, for the night was cold, and the biting east wind seemed to pierce his bones to the very marrow. When within a few yards of the little inn at which he was staying, his arm was touched.

"Buy a box of lights, sir; do buy a box, please!"

He turned. A woman, wretchedly clad, and with death stamped in every feature, stood at his elbow.

"No," answered the clown, roughly; "I don't want any," and he walked on.

But the beggar was not so easily shaken off. She detained him again, and as the wind lulled for a minute, her voice rang in his ear: "Buy a box, sir; just one box!"

At the sound Joe Jeffs turned.

"Let me see your face," he cried hoarsely; then as the pale light of the moon fell upon it: "Nellie, dearie, don't you know me? – Joe, your husband?"

But there was no reply, for his long lost wife lay insensible in his arms.

She was dying, the doctors said – dying of cold and want. So they told her husband, sitting by her bedside in the little inn.

"Can nothing save her?" asked the clown.

"Nothing on earth, my poor fellow – nothing on earth." And the old doctor looked out of the window and blew his nose violently, for the kind-hearted old man was the doctor, and knew something of poor Joe's story, and felt for him.

"Joe."

"Yes, darling."

"Are you sure you quite forgive me?"

A loving kiss was the only answer.

"Nellie, I won't be long," cried the clown.

"Listen!" And by a great effort the dying woman raised herself up; then suddenly: "Joe, dear, what day is it?"

"Christmas Day, Nellie."

"Ah! So it is. More light, for God's sake, more light!"

The doctor made a movement of his hand, and the attendant drew back the curtains from the little window which looked upon the sea, on which lay a broad path of gold, formed of the last rays of the setting sun upon the water.

"How bright it all is, Joe," cried the dying woman, as she sank back upon her pillow. "At last, at last! Joe, darling husband! Good-bye!"

And with a sweet and happy smile on her face, Nellie went down with the sun.

Joe Jeffs still lives at Milford, but he is wonderfully changed, though. People say he is mad, and so he is, in a sad, harmless way. For as sure as Boxing Night comes round, he paints his face and dresses just like clowns do, and there in the little tap-room of the Red Lion he sings Hot Codlins in a little thin cracked voice, and tumbles in a mild and feeble way, and plays a few clownish tricks. How the villagers laugh! They know he is mad, but that doesn't take away from their enjoyment; and one of old Joe's funniest tricks is to address them all as "ladies and gentlemen", and apologise for the non-appearance of the columbine. But when all the merriment is over, old Joe, with his clown's dress still upon him, creeps down, whatever the weather may be, to the little churchyard, where, with his poor old grey head pillowed on a little marble slab inscribed 'Nellie', he pours out a bitter prayer that heaven may take him soon to her he loved so well, and ere he leaves the tomb, with great tears upon his painted face, he softly prays for Nellie too. But the end must soon come.

Each Boxing Night old Joe goes through the same performance, and the people laugh as vociferously as before. But every year he gets more feeble. He can't tumble as he used to, and his sight and memory seem failing fast, and the absent look in his face seems to denote that his thoughts are far away.

And now when people meet old Joe Jeffs, they shake their heads sadly, for they know that soon, very soon, the curtain must fall.

BIBLIOGRAPHY

Newspapers and Magazines:

Brighton Evening Argus; Brighton Guardian; Croydon Advertiser; Croydon Chronicle, Croydon Guardian; Croydon Times; Daily Chronicle; Daily News; Daily Telegraph; Era; Kent Messenger; London Echo; Magnet; Manchester Guardian; Punch; Standard; Times; St James's Gazette; Stage; Sussex Agricultural Express; West Sussex Gazette.

Books:

RD Aldick: *Victorian Studies in Scarlet.*
J Bland: *The Common Hangman: English and Scottish Hangman before the abolition of public executions.* (Hornchurch 1984)
K Chesney: *Victorian Underworld.*
D Donovan: *Suspicion Aroused.* (London 1893)
LS Forbes-Winslow: *Recollections of Forty Years.* (London 1910)
J Goodman: *The Railway Murders.* (London 1984)
L Gribble: *Such was their Guilt.* (John Long 1974)
AGE Jones: *Polar Portraits.* (Caedmon of Whitby 1992)
GHB Logan: *Great Murder Mysteries.* (London 1928)
P Priestley: *Victorian Prison Lives.* (1985)
LTC Rolt: *Red for Danger.* (David and Charles 1978)
A & M Sellwood: *The Victorian Railway Murders.* (David and Charles 1984)
GR Sims: *My Life: Sixty Years of Recollections of Bohemian London.* (London 1917)
HM Walbrook: *Murders and Murder Trials.* (Constable & Co 1932)
JR Whitbread: *The Railway Policeman.* (Harrap 1961)
S Montagu Williams: *Leaves of a Life.* (London 1891)
The Works of Oscar Wilde. (Parragon 1995)

Articles:

An article on Violet Cameron and Lord Lonsdale: *The Observer Magazine* 23/7/1989.
R. Bing: Murderer brings shame on a suburb! (*Wallington and Carshalton Advertiser* 29/11/1979).
Under the reference HO 144 83, I found among other material on the case, Lefroy's autobiography, sub-reference A6404/112a, at the Public Records Office at Kew.